A Recipe for Hope

A Recipe for Hope

Stories of Transformation
by People Struggling with Homelessness

Karen M. Skalitzky

ganesha ✿ books

A RECIPE FOR HOPE
Stories of Transformation by People Struggling with Homelessness
by Karen M. Skalitzky

Edited by L.C. Fiore
Cover design by Tom A. Wright
Text design, interior art and typesetting by Patricia A. Lynch
Photo credit: Steven E. Gross & Associates, Chicago

Published by Ganesha Books, 5443 N. Broadway, Chicago, IL 60640

When necessary, the names of people portrayed in this book have been changed to protect the innocent or in deference to matters legal or private.

ISBN: 978-0-9847907-0-8
Printed in the United States of America

Table of Contents

In gratitude....

Foreword

As you open this book, you enter into a world that may be new to you. But it is not new to the approximately three million Americans who experience homelessness each year, each of whom is a brother, sister, mom, dad, aunt, uncle, son, daughter or friend to someone else. Homelessness is a national tragedy that continues to grow.

I have been privileged to work in the homeless community for the past twelve years. When I began working with the Chicago Coalition for the Homeless [CCH], I had the typical misconceptions and prejudices about the homeless that some readers may also share.

In the 1980s, mentally ill patients were deinstitutionalized, causing communities across the country to experience an influx of people suffering from mental illness. As a result, I initially believed that mental illness was the major cause of homelessness. But I was wrong. At most, only twenty percent of the homeless are mentally ill; the major cause of homelessness is poverty.

But the poor are not the only ones who experience homelessness. Although people in poverty experience homelessness more easily than others, homelessness is not limited to one personality type, race or economic background. The homeless demographic includes inner-city people of color as well as whites from the suburbs, college graduates, and people who once held good jobs. It can affect any and all, and the problem of homelessness impacts everyone, whether they are directly involved with a service organization or not.

Pain and loss have a way of teaching us what we already have, and no one is immune to life's tragedies, heartaches or failures. But what happens to people who lose all of their belongings? What does a person have to hold onto, when all the trappings of money, prestige and property are gone? What is important when all of life's possessions can be carried in a shopping cart? In these stories, you will see the many faces of a problem that is mostly considered a faceless problem, but in them you will find *A Recipe for Hope*, a bittersweet recipe for what is really important. You will be introduced to people who may be homeless but not hopeless, and at the conclusion of each chapter are wonderful recipes that have been submitted by some of Chicago's finest chefs—simple, elegant, delightful, and meant to be shared.

As executive director of CCH, I am often asked to talk about the causes and solutions to homelessness. After all, the mission of our organization is to end homelessness. I always say that the major causes of homelessness are lack of affordable housing, living wage jobs, and social services. All of these require serious commitments by all sectors of our government. The solution to homelessness is not simple, but it is solvable.

After I provide facts, figures, statistics and stories, the question I am asked most is: "How do you respond to a homeless person who asks for money on a street corner?" This is an important question because for many it is the initial experience of coming face to face with someone who is homeless.

The answer I always give is this: simply acknowledge the person, smile, and say, "Hello." The first step to solving homelessness begins with recognizing the humanity in every one of us.

Edward Shurna
Executive Director, Chicago Coalition for the Homeless

Introduction

Some places are so dilapidated and run-down they make you feel like the scum of the earth. Not here. Here it's exotic almost. Makes me want to leave a tip.
— A new guest at The Living Room Cafe

. . .

In the dim light of a winter morning, I drive to Inspiration Cafe. I am welcomed inside; bacon sizzles in the oven and diced tomatoes, yellow squash, green peppers and mushrooms sauté on the stove. Fresh cut flowers, donated by a local grocery store, sit in small vases on each of the twelve tables.

By 6:30 a.m., several pots of coffee are making the rounds. Red plastic mugs and today's *Red Eye* newspaper crowd the tables. Old love songs and Motown favorites play on the radio. I move among the tables, taking orders and refilling juice glasses.

The first orders come out of the kitchen by 7:15 a.m. and continue unabated until 8:30 a.m. Seafood omelets with hollandaise sauce, breakfast burritos, fresh fruit pancakes—strawberry, banana, mango—the choices go on and on.

This is Kevin's first week. He shakes my hand and thanks me for being here. Mary is quick to show me pictures of her new grandbaby. Howard tells bad jokes that make us laugh in spite of ourselves. Janice talks to me about an upcoming job interview. John squeezes my hand and asks about my week. Robert gives me the latest in sports.

In my car again, I sit for a moment, not ready to drive back into my world. I turn on the ignition. Lukewarm air begins to blow through the vents. I see a homeless man standing on the corner. His winter coat looks worn. I can't help but wonder, does he feel like the "scum of the earth?"

Stopped at a major intersection, I watch an older woman hold a battered coffee cup and a cardboard sign that asks for help. Does she gush over her grandbabies too?

In the alley behind my apartment, I drive past a cluster of trashcans and a grocery cart. Plastic bags, aluminum cans and personal belongings stand exposed for all to see. Whose brother, daughter, friend, cousin, uncle is this?

• • •

Homeless. The word has no face, no identity, no future. In Chicago alone, over 166,000 people experience homelessness each year. On any given night, an estimated 9,600 men, women and children make the streets or local shelters their home. Nationally, the numbers catapult to 2.3–3.5 million.[1]

Harry Madix, an eighteen-year veteran of the Chicago Transit Authority [CTA] and the current manager at Inspiration Cafe, explained it best. "You see, Karen. This is how I understand it now: The spirit goes first. Then the mind. And then the body." He was homeless for ten years, walking the streets, not trusting himself, not trusting anyone, until he came to the cafe.

A red Radio Flyer wagon hangs from the cafe ceiling, a testament to possibility. Sixteen years ago that wagon carried sandwiches and coffee up and down the streets of Chicago. Today, three cafes—Inspiration Cafe, The Living Room Cafe and Cafe Too—carry on its message, serving housed and unhoused Chicagoans and changing lives.

Both Inspiration Cafe and The Living Room Cafe offer restaurant-style meals, case management, employment services, cultural events and subsidized housing units as a means for guests (participants) and alumni (graduates) to overcome homelessness and rebuild their lives. Cafe Too, a culinary arts training program and full-service restaurant, offers employment for graduates, as well as breakfast, lunch and dinner to the general public.

• • •

The only thing I knew for sure the first morning I walked through the cafe doors was the promise I'd made to myself: I didn't want anyone to think I wouldn't break bread with them. That was it. I wasn't out to change the world, just to share a meal or two.

Over the next year the meals turned into conversations and I started to ask if anyone wanted to tell their stories. The majority said, "Yes." Some said, "No." I decided to interview anyone who expressed interest—guests, alumni, volunteers and staff—the housed and the unhoused.

We'd meet privately, sit in an empty office or walk to the Weekend Engagement Center during its off-hours.[2] My opening question was always: What does it mean to tell your story? Other questions unfolded as I listened.

Disillusionment and despair, perseverance and hope. I was constantly humbled by their words. Every person I interviewed, despite the complexity of their circumstances and the diversity in education, age, culture and need, spoke of their gratitude and desire to help someone else—a message that rarely makes today's headlines.

I am no stranger to stories of transformation; I have been a literacy specialist in public schools for the past ten years. I spend much of my time in classrooms, observing instruction, talking with students and listening to teachers. I ask teachers to reflect on their practice and then guide them to a deeper understanding of the learning process and their students' needs.

Every year I witness instructional change, rising expectations, and students who begin to excel in schools that have long been considered failures. The thing I've learned the most about change is that you never know the moment it will happen, any more than you know the impact you have on other people.

When I started volunteering three years ago, I had no idea I'd be writing a book. But somehow along the way, this book resurrected me. For that I am deeply grateful, beyond words grateful.

• • •

A *Recipe for Hope* is an invitation to break bread, to savor the insights and ponder the lessons of the men and women you meet. Stories like that of Ms. E. B., whose marriage survives not having a home, speak to resilience and determination in the face of life-altering events. Others, like Tasha and Harry Madix, reflect on the journey and life as they now know it back in mainstream society.

Many voices speak to everyday phenomena: faith, love, family, work, community. Michael Korzun offers us a love story. Jose Contreras, the desire to be a good dad. Gloria Carter, the need to give back. A few describe life on the streets and their need to reclaim their identity, their dignity, their sense of joy. And still others, volunteers and staff alike, share their own transforming experiences.

Eclectic in nature, their stories aren't asking for the proverbial handout or hand-up, but rather a hand*shake*, a willingness to engage, to see, to listen, to be changed. These three cafes and the men and women who gather around their tables give us a window into hope's resilience, its triumph over adversity, and its insatiable hunger for community, respect, and dignity.

• • •

Michael Korzun secured his apartment through the cafe after being homeless for three years. He works downtown and comes to the cafe on his days off to spend time with his friends.

His interview is short, fifteen minutes. It's all about this woman he loves, how they met, how they care for one another, how he worries he's not enough for her. At the end of the interview, I ask him what it means to tell his story.

He tells me, "This is the first time I have someone in my life that really matters to me. That's what it means to tell my story."

I smile. But the truth is I'm disappointed that the interview is all about her. I tell him that his story is like a beautiful picture and we need to frame it with some information about him. He says he'll think about it.

A few weeks later he wants to tell me more. We meet. Once again, it's all about her. I thank him. I tell him I don't think his story will really fit with the book. But I promise to type it up and I decide I'll give it to him as a gift for her.

Months pass. I start working on his tapes. I listen to how they sit by the lake, how he writes her poetry, how he's afraid he's not smart enough for her, how he can't wait to take her out to the theatre like the men and women he sees getting out of taxis downtown, how he has to go to a thrift shop to get a button-down shirt for a wedding they've been invited to.

I am so busy thinking about what a lovely gift this will be for her, I can't even see what a gift Michael's story is for me. I take a break. Go for a walk. And it hits me, stops me cold. When have I ever looked at a man or woman on the street and thought about who they loved?

Never.

Michael's story opened my eyes. We are all human. And we all love.

About the Recipes

We're not just giving you a meal—not just putting calories in your body—we're treating you with dignity and respect and that's a very potent stimulant.

– A weekly volunteer at the cafe

. . .

This book was inspired by Inspiration Corporation and its commitment to end homelessness by maintaining the dignity and respect of everyone it serves. Through a comprehensive array of programs and social services, Inspiration helps men and women rebuild and improve their lives.

Dining with dignity is the essence of Inspiration's philosophy. All of the meals at Inspiration Cafe and The Living Room Cafe are served restaurant-style, with volunteer servers taking individual orders and volunteer cooks working hard to honor their requests. Meatless spaghetti sauce or eggs over medium—nothing is too small to ask.

The same is true with the staff of the Cafe Too restaurant, many of whom are interns from each new graduating class. Serving meals to the public demands the same level of commitment to fine food and customer satisfaction. Dining with dignity serves everyone.

Over the years, many Chicago chefs have woven a web of support for Inspiration. They've prepared delicious meals for guests and alumni, patrons and donors. They've donated countless cooking utensils, pots and pans, and many coveted food items such as fresh shrimp and homemade greens. They've offered insights into and advice about Chicago's expanding culinary world.

To honor their commitment, I asked seven chefs to contribute a favorite recipe, one that is elegant and yet simple to make. Their recipes can be found at the end of each chapter. I hope you savor them as much as I have.

Chapter One

FORTITUDE

"I don't want to just be something that passed."
Michael Purnell

"Every day was like a miracle at the cafe."
Lisa Nigro

"I want to stand up on my own."
Kevin Lancaster

"Whatever it takes."
Deirdre Merriman

✣ Roasted Chicken with Pumpkin and Parsnips ✣
Chef Dominique Tougne

Michael Purnell

It's late May. I find myself sitting across the table from Michael, a tape recorder be-tween us and a broken record playing in my head: What am I doing here? Do I really know how to do this? I've never written a book before. This is crazy.

Michael, with his distinguished looks and silvering hair, just smiles at me. He begins to talk. Eagerly. Effortlessly. This is how I know Michael Purnell. We've talked through many a breakfast at the cafe. His words captivate me and his calm puts me at ease.

I know I'm not alone in this. Everyone at the cafe knows Michael. I've heard his words agitate and shock, soothe and inspire, probe and contend. This morning with the tape recorder is no exception. It's almost as if he's mentoring me. And by the end, I realize I have only one question playing in my head: How can I not write this book?

Before I came to the cafe a couple of years ago, I was sleeping in an alley. Doing crack in a wall that wasn't more than a foot wide. I had to climb in. They used to board it up, you know, trying to keep me out. Only thing they kept out was the wind.

The only thoughts I had were where was I going to get the next hit. I was dead to myself. Literally dead. But it was that realization of self that gave me the motivation to change. That's really what it takes to beat addictions anyway, or to beat anything else: self-motivation.

There are a lot of things—I just sit and think it's God, you know. It's just to say it was just my time. I stopped. I got clean. I came to Inspiration Cafe and attended their Cafe Too program.[1] I worked at the cafe for a while, in various food service positions. And things just started rolling after that. I found permanent employment.

As my head became clearer, I began to do a little introspection. The veil lifted. I stopped fooling myself. Before, you know, it was never my fault. It was always your fault. Somebody told me somewhere along the line that if you don't recognize a problem, you have nothing to work with. So I found out that Michael was a part of the problem.

Now I can sit down and think about things instead of reacting to them. I used to just take it bad. I know my perception of things is not necessarily right. At age fifty-nine, I guess I'm growing. That's beauty. I can see Michael for who Michael is. I don't always like it but I can accept it.

For a long time I wouldn't tell anybody anything. I prayed, "God, what is it you want me to do?" I felt like he kept me here for a reason, you know. To walk through the fire, to get through it and be able to recount to other people what happened, it's a blessing. Truly a blessing.

I have no problem telling you, you're not guaranteed to wake up. God took the time to wake you up this morning. That's why I come up to the cafe—not that I think I'm doing this well—but come on man, if I can do it, you can do it. It's just a matter of applying yourself. All things are possible with that higher power.

I may not be where I want to be, but I'm a long way from where I came. What better testimony is there than that?

Are you familiar with the lotus blossom? It's a rare, beautiful flower that blooms in one of the nastiest places you can possibly think of. So you know, I think that's cool. I am rising from the muck and mire I've created in my life. And I feel blessed to share. My God has brought me a very long way.

I guess the beauty of my position is that I can reach out. I can make my story fit just about anyone. I've been the bad headstrong child. I've been a lawbreaker. An addict. An alcoholic. That's a pretty wide spectrum. I'd want people not to travel the same path.

There is help. For those who are caught up in the madness, there is hope. There are organizations willing to help if you just avail yourself of them. I'm really focused on the youth—that's who I really want to help. They really are the truth and the reality. They're tomorrow.

So my story is for them, but if applicable elsewhere, so be it. I mean, the good kids, I don't worry about them. It's the ones that go in the opposite direction. Those are the ones I really focus on. And, there's a bunch of them…a bunch of them. I just hate to see it.

When I worked for the Salvation Army, they'd send the kids to the kitchen for punishment, make them wash down the walls or clean the stove. And in the process, they were forced to listen to me. I wouldn't sugarcoat anything, especially with the young guys.

A lot of them were hooked up with the gangbangers, all slick, you know. Taboos hold a fascination. So I used to tell them how it is. Most of the stuff they're doing, I've done. It's a total waste of time. It's time you can never actually get back.

That's basically what I want to put out there. Continue doing what you're doing, and if it's the wrong thing, you'll get it. I've been there, done that. And you don't have to go that route. But if you do, and you continue to use drugs, you got three things coming: jail, institution and death. It's a given, not a maybe.

That's the message. Hopefully, if it's said, you'll hear it and won't do it. That's all. I've never really been one to tell others what to do, especially with their lives. I myself resent authority to an extent. I don't like people on my back. I don't want your criticism. But, suggestions I think are a nice way to communicate. They leave your options open.

Just do the next right thing. That's all you can do. Do the next right thing. It truly simplifies things. I wouldn't want anybody to walk in my shoes. I'm scared of them myself. Think I'd set them up on the back porch. I do.

I admit I've made some really bad choices in life. I suffer the repercussions. Society is not as forgiving as we would like. I made some bad choices. I paid my debt. I came back. But now you won't allow me to show you that I'm different.

I'm asking you for a job and you're going to tell me that I can't work because I have a record. I can't get a place to stay because I have a record. I can't even go to school because I have a record. So what is it that you want me to do?

You know, like this neighborhood, it's full of disenfranchised people, for whatever reason. Not all of them are dope fiends. Not all of them are criminals. Some of them are here because of natural disaster. It's on the news almost every day.

Look at the recent flooding in Gurnee.[2] I wonder where those people are right now. With the job market in its present state and high housing prices, where are these people going to go if they don't have major money? They're some of the people you might see up here tomorrow.

I have to ask this question, especially to those who profess belief in God. Even the Bible tells you that when Jesus came they didn't recognize him. So if you see him today, would you recognize him? It could be that person on the corner. It could be that wino. It could be anybody. I get a kick out of that, you know.

In this neighborhood, it's predominantly immigrant. They don't know anything but this neighborhood. Some of them never leave out. This is all they know. This is their support group. Gentrification? Where they going to go? Can they afford housing there?

These are the things people aren't paying attention to. It's about money. I mean, I'm all for property values going up. That's cool. But not at the cost of the human value. And that's the bottom line with everything today. The dollar. You want to tell me that a dollar is worth more than a human life?

I know I'm not unique in my thoughts. But come on, if a lot of people started screaming, something's going to happen. I wonder sometimes, what's the word? Apathy. How can we allow all this stuff to happen with our youth, the schools, housing, this neighborhood? I can go on and on. How can people just not say anything?

Homelessness is a heartbreaking experience. It's a great lesson in humility and humiliation. Your reality is something totally different. You don't have a place to stay. You're hungry. You just walk the streets, no reason why.

Some people break down, totally break down. Become mentally ill as a direct result of being homeless. I've been knowing people in this neighborhood for a long time. And I've been watching some of them just go downhill.

Never had a place to stay. Not looking for a place to stay. I don't know. I think after enough exposure, they just become hopeless. They don't look for anything else. They don't think there *is* anything else.

You were asking me why I want to tell my story. I want to holler. This is my way of hollering. Hopefully, make somebody else holler. You know. How do I say this? You got major surgery and rather than stitches you want to put on a band-aid. It's not happening.

I watch all these organizations. They say, "We have a department here. A de-

24

partment there." Bullshit. The first word that jumps up in my mind is bureaucracy. We got to do this whole thing together because if we don't, we're not doing anything. It's as simple as that.

It has to be holistic. I mean for everything, not just homelessness. I'm talking about the whole shebang. And, it takes everybody. I know it's possible. It can be changed. It has to be.

What can we do to change it?

I have no idea. I can only do what I'm doing now. I can only speak.

What can you do?

Whatever you're best suited for. If you're a teacher, teach. If you're a lawyer, defend. A brickmaker, build houses. Operate in your niche. I don't have the answer. I don't think one person has the answer. But something has got to be done. Buildings are made piece by piece, brick by brick, with the end result a marvelous edification. Do your part. That would be cool.

I'm not perfect. Far from it. I still act crazy. There's still a lot of things I need to work on. But I can look back now and see that I'm a different person. You know, I can feel proud of that. I mean, it's just hope…hope. Without hope, there's just nothing there.

To me, it's like this:

Who am I?	*Michael.*
What am I?	*A child of God.*
Why am I here?	*To spread the word and gather the sheep.*
How, you ask?	*Any way you can.*

Telling my story means there is hope for others. At least I'm hollering and somebody will hear me. I'm not just hollering in my room. Should I leave here tomorrow, I can have the satisfaction of knowing I tried. I tried to shed light where it needed illumination.

I'd like to think I was going toward some type of growth. Come on, you know, let me leave some kind of mark. I don't want to just be something that passed.

Lisa Nigro

Baseball cap worn backwards, faded olive green sweatshirt, blue jeans and tennis shoes, Lisa huddles with her family. "Okay," I hear her say. "This is how you take breakfast orders."

Her husband nods while their son and daughter, thirteen-year-old twins, study the Friday morning menu. At forty-five, Lisa has founded several nonprofits, Inspiration Cafe being the first, sixteen years ago.

We all serve breakfast together. Lisa weaves in and out of the tables, a pot of steaming coffee in hand, refilling mugs and catching up with alumni. Later when I tell her about this project, she links her arm in mine, smiles a warm smile, and agrees. Weeks pass, and we meet again, this time sitting in two red leather chairs next to the windows in her brightly painted family room. This is her story.

My mother was an alcoholic. In third grade I was taken from her to live with my father, and I was thinking, "Okay, I'm in a good place now, away from bad people, from being touched in bad ways, from having violence in the house."

Lisa D. was my friend. One day we were in gym class, changing our clothes, and I see on her leg, she has the *exact* belt buckle, like you could see the bruise but it's a belt buckle. The exact print.

So we devise a plan to rescue her. Get her out. She brings her clothes to school and after school, she doesn't go home. She comes to our apartment. And I'm totally convinced that my father will rescue her because he rescued me, right? So she stays for dinner. But then he says, "It's time for Lisa to go home."

And I'm like, "She's not going home."

"What do you mean she's not going? She has to go home."

"Well no, because…." and I show him her leg. Her belt buckle. And we're both standing there, totally convinced that he's going to do something.

And he says, "Honey, she has to go home."

"But D-ad? She's being beat."

"Lisa, she has to go home."

He calls her mother, and her mother comes—this is the thing I'll always re-member, too—and she's like, "Thank you for having her for dinner…." A total bullshit conversation. And the minute she leaves, my father closes the door, looks at me and says, "Oh, she's a nice lady."

I hear someone tumbling down the hallway. So I open the door and Lisa's be-ing beat to snot all the way down the hall. I turned around, looked at my dad and screamed, "You suck."

And that's the moment I decided all adults are in cahoots. You can't trust them. Forget it. You can't trust anybody.

• • •

The cafe was born out of a nagging feeling I've had ever since I was a little girl, about being put in a position of feeling smaller. That's what society wants you to think.

I come from a family that didn't have money, didn't have power. We had alco-hol and drugs and chaos and poor choices. And because of all that, I was always watching adults act really ridiculous and knowing, even as a little girl, that they could make better choices, that I don't have to live by the rules they're giving me.

But I was always wondering, "How come they don't know they can change their mind?"

• • •

When I became a police officer, I already knew there's crime and there's drugs and there's people who make choices that are idiotic and you have to arrest them. I already knew all that black and white stuff. But the gray….

I see a lot of things that aren't going to be reported to the police. You just know people are going to take care of their own stuff. It's called street justice. So I gath-ered information about social services agencies and I'd go to the person in the family and say, "I know you're not going to sign a police report, but here's some information." Not really saying that a particular thing was going on, but just giving them information.

For example, I came to a shooting one day, a man got his testicles shot. He's in bed and there's screaming and there's blood but no one is going to sign a complaint. They just said an "unknown assailant" came in and shot him. And I was like, no. Something bad happened here.

So I talked to the matriarch of the family and I said, "I know you're not signing a police report but here's some information about child abuse, rape and different things." My sergeant was standing there and heard this. We left. We made a police report. That was it.

I came back into the station. The shit hit the fan. "You're *not* a social worker. You're a police officer."

What else are you going to do? We both know nothing's going to happen. They're not going to sign anything. I'm sure that man was raping some little boy and the matriarch probably shot him. You know. But the kid didn't need to suffer and the family needs information.

And this happened over and over and over again, to the point where finally I got some backlash from my tribe of policemen. They were like, "If you're not going to play our game, then you're going to be putting yourself in danger." And that's pretty much what started happening. I wasn't getting back-up when I needed it, because I wasn't playing the game.

So I had to make a decision. Do I really want to be a police officer? I started thinking about injustice and I read an article in the paper about a cafe in Atlanta. They serve homeless men and women with dignity and respect, and I thought that was a pretty cool way of treating people.

I took a leave of absence and told my husband Perry that I wanted to go down there, and he said, "Let's go." So we drove down to Atlanta. They'd had a lot of people visit so they were kind of like, "If you really want to do this, then it's yours." They trained us for one day, and then we pretty much ran the cafe for the next two.

It was so great. I loved it. Perry, who's really introverted and quiet, he was forced to participate in the mix. And I was like, "Wow. That's a miracle." So driving home, we're like, "We're inspired." And that's how Inspiration Cafe came to be.

• • •

We came back to Chicago and I was all excited. But people know me. I'm the person who always has ideas and so people were like, "Oh, Lisa's on another little whim. Where's she going this time?"

And I kept saying, "No. *No*. I'm doing this. This is what's happening."

So I borrowed my nephew's Radio Flyer wagon and I put in bagels and cream cheese and coffee—I had a promise. Perry and I, we love coffee. We want good coffee. Not shelter coffee, which tends to be watered-down. We always got good coffee, pre-Starbucks good coffee.

And we went out on the street in Uptown. Lisa Madigan, Ester Hall, Vanessa Rich and myself. We just started pulling the wagon around, serving coffee and sandwiches and bagels, on our own, just talking to people. And we got very popular. People loved the coffee and the fact that we didn't make them listen to a sermon or do anything to get it.

So then I rigged the back of my Isuzu Rodeo with catering equipment so we could cook the food, put it in my car and keep it hot. Eggs benedict on the street was my favorite. It was fabulous. We served quiche Lorraine, egg McMuffin sandwiches, like our own little thing. And always right outside the Salvation Army on Sunnyside and Broadway.

Then someone told me about this guy, Pastor Paul, he's like the Pied Piper of food. I went to see him in Minnesota. He convinced truckers who couldn't get to their destinations on time to bring the food to his church and he'd take it into the projects.

So there we are handing out sacks of potatoes and big bushels of vegetables, all this fresh food. No one was mean. They stood in line. They were so nice and so grateful. The little kids were just like dying for an apple. And we're in the United States of America.

I was just like, "What? This is so incredible. I can't even believe it." And he just did it. That's the best part. You just do it. He's the one who gave me the idea to have a mobile cafe.

I came back to Chicago and a friend of mine, Jan Baccus, she knew this guy who owned this church who had this bus who wanted to donate it. I took all the chairs out and my friends who were carpenters built it out to be a restaurant.

People couldn't believe it. We still brought all the dishes with us. Washed them at my house. Got up the next morning—five o'clock—to cook whatever we had. Me and my family. Every breakfast, every day. We'd serve maybe fifteen people at a time inside and then we had coffee and Danishes for the people outside.

Only it was really short-lived because someone in the neighborhood called Channel Nine. They did a story on me. And this guy who owned a huge apartment building, Peter Holsten, he saw me on TV and said, "I'll give you six months free." It was just a little office space, but I was like, this is so great. 1319 West Wilson. Signed the lease on my thirtieth birthday.

My friend Vicki Dalicandro asked if she could help me and I said sure. She was needing something in her life and to this day, her husband—my husband already knew I was crazy—but her husband still says he's never seen anybody just pop out of bed at 5:00 a.m. We were flying by the seat of our pants. Running on pure positive energy all the time.

Before we got a stove, we did everything out of a big restaurant wok. It was so low-key. Just regular household equipment. And then someone would feel sorry for us and they'd find me the next thing I needed. I got a walk-in freezer donated. Tables and chairs. Toys. Books.

And the interesting thing about the cafe, when I opened the new space, it was going to be for women and children. I got a few, but only a few. And I couldn't figure it out. They told me, "We get a lot of our needs met in the area. You know who really needs your help? The guys."

I was like, "You're kidding. But if you think so, put it out there."

The next day the place was full. It went from five people to like thirty people in a day.

• • •

Every day was like a miracle at the cafe. There was no staff. The phone rang morning to night. One of the guests, Tim, said, "I'll take your phone calls if you allow me to stay overnight in the cafe."

And in my mind I'm thinking, "Oh my God, he's going to leave the door open or they're going to be shooting heroin and I'm gonna lose my dream." But you have to have faith. If you really believe in what you're doing, you have to have faith.

I was totally sweating when I gave Tim the keys. He could have done anything, but he didn't. He took all the phone calls. He made sure the next morning was set up. It was a dream. I couldn't pay him a salary but I realized I could raise money for his rent. So we got him an apartment upstairs. That and cigarettes were his stipend.

We were doing all kinds of fundraisers, catering mostly. Me and Perry's mom. We'd never catered in our life. We'd go to the library and find these restaurant books and crank out these wild meals. And every single time it was a success. I mean, every single time.

That's why, even today, I for sure, one hundred percent know that the cafe is totally driven by something bigger than us. There's no way. I mean like, we catered some crazy chili cook-off. We were all dressed in western wear. We had cornbread coming out our butt, and people just kept coming out of nowhere. It was…it was a true miracle.

And we were never out of food. People would drop off food from the floor to the ceiling at the cafe. All the time. They'd heard me on the radio with Studs Terkel, or they saw me on TV. I didn't want to refuse anybody giving me donations so I just gave it away. It was like a mania. A crazy, happy mania.

I'd also been given a public relations person, Laurie Glenn, along with the six months free. So we got local celebrities to come and serve a meal in the cafe. The City of Chicago came with its film crew, but they had to pull me aside because it was totally illegal.

I had no idea. I had my sanitation license. But I didn't know you needed a huge ventilator hood. So they filmed the event, but they didn't film the kitchen. And then they said, "We're going to give you ten thousand dollars to do the hood."

That's how you know it was a miracle. I mean, come on.

. . .

For me, it all changed when we hired staff. That's when I started evolving out. It was late in my pregnancy and I had to become a different person, you know, be the manager. The problem-solver.

When it was just me kind of flitting around, I didn't have to worry about anybody but myself. If I screw up, it's on me. But if I put all my faith in something and someone else screws up, I take it personally. And you can't do that in business.

It's like a life lesson for me. Who can I trust? I know it comes from my childhood. I have to take little leaps of faith every day. Just like doing little things and saying to myself, "I'm going to let this go." Like giving money to a panhandler on the street.

One time I wouldn't give money to someone because I knew he was a user. My mother, who used to use drugs really bad, looked at me and said, "Why do you care what he uses it for?"

And I was like, "Why would I give him money to go use what's totally destroying him?"

"Because you've never had withdrawal symptoms in your *whole* life. You don't know what it's like when your body's violently ill, when you're shaking, everything's spinning, and you can't stop it, and you're totally scared."

And when she told it like that, I was like, "Oh my God." It's not really as complicated as we make it. Anybody can be sitting in a chair in the cafe. I've had high school friends of mine who are homeless, not knowing it was me, walk through the cafe. I've had former bosses who became junkies and I've served them at the cafe. It could be me.

The cafe's really more about a feeling, how we're all just people eating breakfast together, hanging out. Like, let's say you have schizophrenia and you're always going to treatment and you want to show your appreciation to your counselors but you can't. You're homeless.

You can invite them to the cafe. It's like your place. And, now you have an even playing field to talk. Person to person.

That's how I always thought about it. That each person sitting there is my uncle or my father or my mother…. And there's lots of people who didn't make it. Lots of people who died because they went back out on the streets.

• • •

Eight years ago, we were asked to go to Russia to start the cafe the same way it started in Chicago. Russia was changing to democracy and it totally crashed. Tons of kids were on the street. There were no shelters. And this Christian organization wanted to serve them. So I said I'd go but I wanted Harry Rogers to go with me. I knew I'd be safe with him.

Harry came into my life back when we were just starting to hire staff. Another guest who worked for us, Richard, suggested we hire him. He told me Harry used to be a con artist, but he'd been drug free for a long time and he really understood the guests.

I said, "Dude. You're bringing somebody who steals for their life into the cafe? Into my whole world?" I wasn't walking my faith at all. But I really liked Harry, so I told Richard, "I'll hire him, but if he steals one thing, a paperclip, you're fired. And he's fired too."

And I was totally ashamed in the end. Harry was the most respected, most influential staff member we had. He was so meticulous about everything. He wanted to make sure I'd always trust him. And I told him the truth, "You made me realize there is potential to change."

So Harry and I go to Russia with this organization. And we smuggle in all these school supplies in our restaurant equipment. We're in the airport in Moscow, everybody's getting their stuff checked and they just walked us through. I swear it was another miracle. No mafia guys met us anywhere.

And while we're there we taught them how to set up the equipment and keep everything sanitized, but the government started to see what we were doing. So we went into the forest. We had this big barbeque. And it started to rain. But the kids were just joyous. They were singing and running around.

And right as all this was going on, we hear twigs breaking. These guys with machine guns come up and they surround us. I'm sweating. Totally shaking. This is it. We're going to be killed right here in the forest and no one will ever know. Who would know? They take your passports at the hotel and we didn't tell the embassy we were coming because we were smuggling in school supplies.

So they're coming toward us, and I grab Harry's hand and I say, "Harry, pray with me right now. Just pray with me." So we're both standing there, in the rain, in Moscow, praying as hard as we can, and they didn't ask us a thing. They walked away.

It had to be God. It's so God, I can't even believe it.

The cafe's in Russia. Isn't that crazy?

• • •

Every interview you read about me, the reporters always twist it. They say my heart's always been with the poor and that makes sense to people. But the cafe didn't come from that place. It didn't come from some happy, loving, joyful place.

The cafe was born out of me being pissed off at the world, the way it is and the rules of society. It's like a seed planted in love that—even though it came from a dark place—grew into something beautiful. What mother wouldn't take a dandelion necklace from her kid even though you want to kill them all in your yard?

The cafe came from a dark place. And I'm okay with that. God made dark and light. And, the cafe is a total place of light. That's what it is.

This one time we didn't have any money. The president of the board said if we didn't get money soon, we'd have to close down. I turned to Frank Lott who was a minister on the board with me, and I said, "Hey Frank, let's pray about this."

The board was like, "You're crazy. You're praying for money?"

And I said, "Yes, we're praying for money."

A week later we got unsolicited funds of twenty thousand dollars. And if you ask the board how that happened, they'll say it was luck.

But there's no way. Those unsolicited funds came from prayer, from hope, from knowing it was going to happen. That's what I think. And that's what it means to tell my story.

Kevin Lancaster

In his faded jeans, leather jacket and wool scarf, Kevin slides into the passenger seat. His grandson's basketball game is about to start. It's early evening. The winter sky is already dark. I pull away from the curb and the cafe slowly disappears from view.

Kevin Lancaster is fifty-one. He grew up in South Shore but has since traveled all over the United States and Europe. He hopes to touch the pyramids one day.

I've been with The Living Room Cafe close to eight months now. I was very discouraged at the time I came. I had no money. No home. No transportation. I'd just left a perfectly good job and here I was, almost on the streets. I was like, "What happened?"

I guess that's the chance you take. When you go for it, sometimes you win. And sometimes you lose. This is one of the times I lost.

I was working for a well-known collection agency. And this friend of mine— we'd known each other for like twenty-some years—he wanted to open a medical billing practice in Atlanta. So he says, "I know you can do this. I need you to come down here and get the system set up. I'll put you in the Marriott. Get you a car. Pay you six hundred dollars a week."

So I left. Went down to Atlanta. I'd lived there before and had always wanted to return. This was an opportunity of a lifetime. I was like, "I'm *out* of here." You know.

I get down there and I'm getting everything set up. We go pick out the office, nice location, everything. My friend, he was working to obtain a license but he couldn't get it. He couldn't get the license. So…so that…that killed that.

I'd been under the impression I was getting ready to be the manager, you know. I was looking at condos and places to invest my money. Figuring like in a year's time, I'd be sitting pretty good. But that didn't happen. And it killed me.

I ended up coming back to Chicago with nothing. I was so distraught. Didn't really have a place to live. I was staying with some friends but they could only put me up for so long. I ended up staying with the mother of some people I knew. She needed money. I needed a place.

But I was scraping just to pay rent on a weekly basis. I was one step away from being on the streets. I went to a financial aide office and they referred me to Inspiration Corporation. At first, I was like, "Yeah, right. Inspiration Corporation? Ok-ay, fine."

But being in the dire situation I was in, I figured what the heck. And to my surprise, people were very friendly. Very open. Very personal. Totally the opposite of the financial aide office. Their attitude is like, "Look. I got a job. I got mine. You get yours." They don't really care about you. You're just a number.

I'm really grateful for The Living Room Cafe. It was difficult bouncing around, not really having a permanent home, address, or even a phone number for employers to contact me. It wasn't that I was unemployable—I was just never stable long enough for them to contact me. And by the time I contacted them, the job was already filled.

The cafe gave me transportation, a place to stay, voicemail and lots of encouragement. They give you all the support in the world. Furniture, food, utensils. Everything you need to run a household. It's not the most lavish place, but it's comfortable. And having your own place has a lot to do with you being creative. Inspired. Determined.

You really can't focus on getting ahead if you have no place to lay your head. What are you going to do if you're out on the streets? I mean, it's not likely that you're going to find a substantial job. You'll find a fast-food job or some grunt work. But you won't last because it's not something you want to do. At least I won't.

The last few months, I've been doing temp jobs. A month here. Two weeks there. But now I'm a little more focused on getting something I can retire from. It looks good. Two positions are pending. One is a claims analyst position. I'd be the liaison between the patients and the hospital. The other is with a surgeon who's setting up his own practice. I'd be in billing and collections.

They're both kind of high-profile jobs, something where you got to think rather than just do. It's not like working on an assembly line, which is something I have a desperate hate for. I'm hoping to get my own home-based business started. That's my goal. Hopefully within the next five years, that can be obtained. I just need a job to get back on the road.

I owe this place a lot. There are some great people here and they seem to have a legitimate interest in me and what I want to do. I really appreciate that. No one owes you anything. And for people to care about your goals and objectives, that's valued more so than anything else. It really boosts your morale, your determination, your focus on how to get there.

I'm really looking forward to when I become an alum and I can give something back to The Living Room Cafe. I want to help people in here the way I was helped. Maybe just be like an advisor, you know. You can go see Kevin and he'll help you get a job.

Hopefully, someone will benefit from my story. That's my purpose for doing this. I know it's just a matter of time for me. The thing is, though, how long can you hang on and be in your right mind? If you've always been self-sufficient, it's difficult depending on someone else for such vital things as food and rent. I'm not accustomed to it. And it worries me.

I know I can do better. I don't want to have to depend on Inspiration Corporation to take care of me. That's on my mind all the time. I'm always thinking of ways to try to get out of all this. Not that I don't appreciate it, but I'll feel better about myself—better attitude, better outlook—if I'm more independent.

I know you're not meant to go through it alone, but you should be able to stand up on your own. Food, shelter, clothing, things you'd think should be a given. That's what I'm talking about. I want to stand up on my own.

Deirdre Merriman

"Quit looking at me like I'm some kind of saint," Dee says with a laugh. She runs her hand through her hair as I blink my way back to the conversation. I decide I better tell her I'd been busy thinking about a teacher I know who always tells me that teaching is the easiest part of her day because that's when she forgets she's handicapped.

Dee concurs and shifts quietly in her motorized wheelchair. "There isn't anything I can't do. The only thing I can't do is walk. Everything else I can do. I might do it differently, but I can do it." She lets the words sink in. "I know there will come a day when my body will give out, but until then, there isn't anything I can't do."

I look at her Winnie the Pooh jean jacket and her Starbucks coffee mug, and realize it's hard not to be humbled in her presence.

I want you to use my name. It's important. Not because I'm important or because what I've achieved in my life is important particularly, but because I think it's important for people to know it can be done.

I never believed it. Never in a million years would I have believed that I'd be changed in the way I am now. When I was homeless and drinking and living under the bridge, I'd wish for a life like I have now. But I never had any belief that I could achieve it.

And now that I have, it's like—it is a miracle, you know. I think people need to know that if I can do it—I heard that phrase too and I hate to say that, "If I can do it, anyone can do it." It's a cliché. That's what people say all the time. But it's true. That's the thing about clichés. There's always a grain of truth in them, however trite they sound.

I was born in Ireland. My parents were alcoholics. My father abused me in every way. He left us when I was thirteen, and my mum got sober when I was eleven. I was gang raped as a teenager in front of my brothers. Was raped again. And then in my own little career, my husband died worrying about my drinking. My children were three and one at the time.

I lost my children because of my drinking. Lost my home because of my drinking. Lost everything because of my drinking. And I continued to drink anyway. I had my neck broken and I'm in a wheelchair because of my drinking. It was domestic violence but I wouldn't have been in the situation if I hadn't been drinking. So I had nothing. Nothing.

And yet here I am today sober. I have no real reason. There was no real motivation behind me getting sober. No driving force or reward at the end of the tunnel or anything else. It's just—well, I think it was God, myself. That's a personal thing, I suppose. Not everyone believes in God, but I believe in God. Not in religion, but in God.

I continued drinking after my neck was broken. I was an alcoholic. I drank. That's what alcoholics do. And I wasn't willing or able to do anything about it at the time. I was at a party with free beer. Best kind of party there could be for an alcoholic—free beer. I drank half of my beer. Turned to my friend and said, "Take me to the emergency room."

"Why? What's wrong?"

"Don't worry about it. Just take me to the emergency room."

I didn't know why I was going. Two months before that, I'd attempted suicide. Spent two weeks in a nut ward. I went to the same emergency room and said, "I'm feeling suicidal again," which I kind of was. But this time I added, "And by the way, I have a drinking problem."

I don't even know where that came from. But I knew it was the right thing to do. That was on my daughter's birthday. Day of my daughter's birthday was the day I had my last drink.

I didn't realize it at the time. At the time I was focused solely on getting to where I was going. Because at that point, once I made the decision, I was willing to do whatever it took. Whatever I had to do to get sober and stay sober. Getting sober is easy. Staying sober is hard. I was determined. Focused. I had to do whatever it took. Whatever it took. And it took a lot.

Later on I realized, "My God, that was Louise's birthday." I kind of like that. Every time it's her birthday, it's my anniversary. She and I are talking again. In fact we have a great relationship again, which is more than I deserve but I'm delighted.

Life is good.

People need to know that it's not what life deals you, it's how you deal with what life deals you. And there's nothing you can't deal with. There really isn't. You might not see how at the time but if you wait long enough, you will. You'll get through it. It's just a question of how. Are you going to fight? Are you going to figure out a way to get through it? Are you going to give up? What do you want to do? That's your decision. Your responsibility.

Everyone runs around blaming other people for everything. But you can't. You're just causing yourself more problems. I should speak for myself. I look at my problems now as challenges. All right, here's the next problem. What are we going to do about this one? That's how I live, basically.

I have a good life. I enjoy living my life. I have everything I need. Not everything I want, but everything I need. I have these moments where everything is okay and I get this flash of just busting-out-of-yourself joy. Do you know what I mean?

It's at those moments that I realize how lucky I am. Lots of things happen that make me realize that. Like when I'm in my room at the nursing home and it's freezing cold in January and the snow's piling down and there's people going by with blankets and pillows under their arms. That was me.

My heart goes out to these people. I know what they're suffering. And like the people in the nursing home who aren't able to fight for themselves, who maybe don't even know that they're being mistreated, you know. I'm lucky. I can fight for myself. And I can fight for other people who can't.

I believe that's what we're supposed to do. And I like it. I think one of my best features, if you like, is that I can put myself into other people's shoes. Thank God for that. To be able to say, "I know how you feel." And mostly, I've had so many experiences in my life, I do know how the person feels. I'm not just saying it.

When I break things down and think about it, I have food. A roof over my head. A bed to go to at nighttime. I have friends. Support. A family again—one that loves me and I allow to love me. I mean, no matter what happens to me, there is always someone somewhere who is going to help me out or help me over the hump.

And now I can actually ask for help. It's difficult for me to do and I get very embarrassed doing it, but I do it. Those are two things that are really important. I'm able to ask for help and I am able to allow people to like me or love me. That took me years to learn. Years to learn. It took me forty-five years to become a person that I could like.

My parents married because of me. As a child of two alcoholics, you always think it's your fault, that there's something wrong with you. I mean, I knew there was something wrong in my family but I had no idea what it was. So by childish logic, it must have been my fault.

My father sexually abused me all the way along until I was gang raped. And after that, he never touched me again. Now this is going to sound stupid but in a thirteen-year-old logical mind, he didn't touch me anymore because I was no good. All I wanted was for him to love me. And I knew he didn't.

You'll find this with all children sexually abused. If that was the only way you could get love—even though it wasn't love, but to you it was—if that was the only way you could get some kind of attention, then that's what you did. And then if both parents…then it had to be your fault. Otherwise, why would they be beating you?

So when you grow up, it's not a question of believing you're no good. You know you're no good. And you know you've never been any good because there's never been a day when you felt like you were any good, or anyone told you that you were any good.

So for most of my life, especially my drinking career, I was no good. Didn't deserve it. Wasn't worth it. An aberration of nature, you know. That's what I believed. Totally believed. It wasn't even an issue. Just part of who you are. Same as breathing. You just know.

And when my mum got sober and everything, I couldn't—even though she would love me and she did love me, and I know now loved me all the way through, even when she was drinking, and know particularly because of my own situation with my children—I wasn't able to feel the love.

I didn't know how. I had this shell around me like a rock-solid ton of lead. If you don't let them see you hurt, then they can't get you. This was me. In fact, the first time I went home ten years ago, my mum and I talked about that. We were talking about my drinking and my difficulties, and she said, "I always loved you."

I cried. I know she did. I know she always loved me and I told her that. But I couldn't feel it, you know. Just couldn't feel it. I had no idea how to love. That's a terrible thing to happen to anybody, especially a child. So basically from the beginning of my life, I never ever, ever felt love. Never felt important. Never felt like I mattered. I just felt like a…a big mistake.

• • •

See, that's part of why my recovery was so difficult. After I was in the hospital for two more weeks, in the nut ward—I loved that nut ward—I went to this very nice treatment program in the suburbs. It was far too nice for what I needed.

While I was there, they diagnosed me as manic-depressive. I was delighted. There's something we can tackle. Now we can treat it. Now we can move on. For me it was great. Because all my life—I remember saying one time, in front of my father, that I was depressed. I was a teenager.

I remember him looking at me and saying, "Don't be so stupid. How could you be depressed? What have you got to be depressed about?"

I never used the word again. Never. I never said I was depressed. Ever. So when the doctor said this, I was delighted. And sure enough, I monitor my condition and everything, but really it doesn't show because I take my meds.

I spent twenty-eight days there, sort of a luxury place, and I knew it wasn't what I needed at all. I needed my ass kicked. Whatever it takes. This nice little place was like the tip of the iceberg. A lot more had to be done. I don't know how I knew, I just knew.

So I asked my counselor, "What is the roughest, toughest place you can go?" I was scared stiff asking all of this, but I knew in my gut what I had to do.

"Gateways in Chicago."

"Is that bad?"

"Real bad."

"All right then, get me a place."

So she called and she called. My public aid was pending, so I had that against me. And I decided to hell with it. I was going to take the bull by the horns. So I called myself. And they gave me the runaround. To cut a long story short, I ended up talking to the director. Time was getting close. I think it was a Friday.

"Look. Here's the situation. I'm leaving this place on Monday. I'm not going anywhere. I'm not passing 'Go.' I'm not collecting two hundred dollars. I will be in your place by Monday afternoon. You might as well have a bed because I'm not leaving. It's that simple. Goodbye."

That's what I did. I went straight there. The director asked me why and all the rest of it. So I said, "I have to do whatever it takes and I know in my gut that this is where I need to be."

"Why? What have you heard about here?"

"I heard it's the nastiest possible place to be."

"Short of prison, I suppose it is."

Inside I'm shaking like a leaf, but I have this macho face going on. Everyone has told me I'm going to be beaten up, mugged, raped. All kinds of bad things will happen to me because I have no street smarts. So I'm scared on the inside and cocky as hell on the outside, which I'm very good at to this day.

And he says, "All right then."

They put me in what is called a MISA program, Mental Illness Substance Abuse. They treat both disorders. That was a twenty-eight-day program, a little bit less nice than before, but it wasn't gut level. I wasn't there yet.

I found out they have a ninety-day program solely for addiction. It's in the same building and everything else. So they kept me in the thirty-day program to wait for a bed in the ninety-day program. And then I went into the ninety-day program.

Holy cow. Oh my God, it was dreadful. Dreadful. They took all my cockiness. No more of this pretending to be wonderful, fine on the outside but not on the inside. No. No. No. None of this was happening, which was exactly the way it should be. 'Course, by the time I started going through that I was kind of like changing my mind here. You know, wait a minute….

But then I realized I was going through it. And I was getting there. I'd keep going up to this one counselor all the time. He was a South African man and he was fantastic. I'd go up to him and I'd say, "I've got it."

"Well what is it?"

I'd explain, and he'd shake his head. "Nope. You haven't got it yet."

Back I'd go. I'd do some more work in the program. And then I'd go back. "I've got it."

"Nope," he'd say. "You haven't got it yet."

I was so frustrated because I wanted it so badly, you know. I was like, "What is it?"

He said, "You'll know when you get it."

This went on for a while. I just kept doing my thing and one day he came to me and said, "You got it."

"I got it?"

"Yes. You got it."

And I said, "So what is it and how do I keep it?" Typical. Totally typical alco-holic. *What is it and how do I keep it?* You know. So I don't lose it.

"It's not a question of that," he told me. "Now that you've got it, you'll never lose it."

I still don't know what it is, but I got it. And apparently I still have it because I'm still sober. It was just so funny. I got it? Now what is it and how do I keep it?

• • •

By this time, I'd already gotten off the street. I moved into a halfway house for people with my problem, which was great. At that time I was walking on a cane and I started falling and breaking bones and stuff. They don't have any medical coverage over there. So they were like, "Really, Dee you can't." That's how I ended up in the nursing home.

So that's what I did to get sober. But then, everybody was talking about ninety Al-coholics Anonymous meetings in ninety days. I'd heard about it before and of course I wasn't willing to do it. But this time I was back to my "whatever it takes" thing. I was like, "Ah, hell. That's a meeting a day. That means I have to get out of bed, go to the meeting, sit there, come back home. I'd miss television and blah, blah, blah."

Somebody said to me, "Well you'd do that if you were going for a beer."

"Yeah I would," I said. "But that doesn't count. I'm not going for beer."

But I did it. Ninety meetings in ninety days. One a day. Every day. I did it.

At the meetings, they tell you there are four promises named for you when you get sober. One of them is that things beyond your wildest dreams will happen. I'd sit in the meetings and listen to these people talking about their wildest dreams having come true and I'd be very happy for them. But I never included myself in that. All I was concerned about was that I was sober. That was fine with me. Wasn't a wildest dreams thing, but that was all right.

Then one day it hit me: I had a home. I was going to college. I was doing all these things and I was sober. If somebody had told me that when I was living under a bridge watching the snow falling, freezing to death, no food, no nothing, I'd have laughed at them, "Excuse me? There is no way on earth."

The mistake I made is that I was thinking about my wildest dreams now. But it's not that. It's your wildest dreams when you're drinking. Things that would have just been totally inconceivable to you when you're in the throes of your alcoholism will come true if you stop drinking. You know? I mean, I'm a success. I'm a big old success story and I know I am. And I'm delighted.

But you see, you also change as you grow. You really do. When I started becoming a success, I was terrified of doing anything wrong. It was back to the old insecurity. Back to the "it." I have to keep this success. "Dear God, I better not do anything wrong. Everyone will know that I'm a big fake."

But every year you progress. I don't worry anymore about keeping this success. I know who I am and I know I'm a success. I'm not drinking and that automatically makes me a success. Right there. Everything else that comes with it makes me even more successful.

And I'm lucky. I'm very lucky to have gotten it. It's a pity I got it so late, but I'm lucky I got it at all. I do have a good life. I mean shit happens, but shit happens in everybody's life. You know. What's the big deal?

So now, I'm finishing my associate's degree in psychology. I was at the student government awards last year and you know the way awards things go on and on and on and you really stop listening? You just clap when everyone else starts clapping. "It's all very nice. Can I go home now?"

Well, they were going on and on about this person who everybody admired. She's always involved in school activities. Always has time to give advice or help somebody with a problem. So on and so forth. And I was thinking, "Who in the hell is this person?"

And the next thing they say is Deirdre Merriman. Well where is she? You know. I'm looking for her. And then I suddenly realize, "Oh shit. That's me."

My advisor is saying, "Dee. Go up there. It's an award for you."

"That's right. It's me." So up I go.

And it's not the award. I don't care so much about that. It was…it was genuine. I'd really been and really done the things they were acknowledging me for. And I realized I didn't have to do all that drinking. If I had just been myself all along, people would have liked me.

When I went home, I put together a big old scrapbook for my mum with like school achievements and certificates. I was looking at it as I was putting it together, thinking, "God, I've done a lot." In five years, I have. Come a long way.

• • •

It's about letting go. Not being so intense about everything. Everything is not life or death, and you're not responsible for every single thing that happens. You're only responsible for what happens to you. And if people happen to see the real you, you won't fall apart. It's okay to be yourself. Even if parts of you are bad, it's still okay. That's what *it* is.

Drinking and addiction are all about fear. You're afraid to be yourself. Afraid of what other people will think of you. Afraid people will see you as you really are and know that you're a fraud. You believe you are. So you're afraid. Insecure. You're all screwed up. And in order to cover all of that, and in order for you yourself to be able to deal with it, you drink. So you can't feel. That's the main thing. Not feeling.

I thought if I relaxed enough to be myself, I'd fall into all these millions of pieces because I was just holding on by my fingernails. And if anybody saw how I really was, they'd start laughing at me. Who do you think you are? What gives you the right to be a human being?

Which all sounds really stupid now, but it was really real at the time. I was terrified of being me. And if I didn't like me, then how the hell could I expect anyone else to? I didn't want anyone to find out what a bad person I was and how undeserving I was.

Which takes me back to my childhood. You can argue that addiction is hereditary. You can say what chance did I have with two parents as addicts? There are five children in the family and out of the five, three of us are addicts. Two in recovery, thank God. One still fighting the battle. I think it's evidence of at least a predisposition.

But the thing that addicts should know, and need to know, is that it's not their fault. It's not their fault they're addicts. What I choose to do about my addiction is my responsibility. But God help me, it's not my fault I'm an alcoholic. I definitely did not volunteer to be an alcoholic. Nobody would. The pain involved is unimaginable.

A lot of people say drugs are different than alcohol. I think in some ways they are, but the bottom line is: addiction is addiction is addiction. It's all about fear and insecurity. You're afraid to feel. Your feelings are so intense. I was afraid to let all that pain go. To be vulnerable. To be hurt. It was much easier to go around pretending everything was okay. I was drunk. Didn't have to feel anything.

Not saying, of course, that I was making a complete fool of myself and also adding to the feelings because after being drunk, I'd feel bad about the stupid stuff I did. I'd get drunk again so I didn't have to feel stupid for being drunk the time before. And so it goes. You're in the vicious cycle. The ideal would be to be permanently drunk.

When I was homeless, that's what it was about. The main focus was getting enough money to get a beer. And then of course, once you got the beer you drank it. But as you're drinking it, you're wondering how you're going to get money to get more beer. Dreadful. Dreadful thing.

And all you really had to do was put down the beer. Such a simple thing. Four words: Put down your beer. But that was so hard to do. Look at how many millions of people can't. The fear is too great.

Beer is my crutch. It's my best friend. Drugs, alcohol, whatever it is, it's your best friend. Always there for you. Never criticizes you. Never talks back. Never fights with you. Supports you. Comforts you. It's the best friend you'll ever have in the whole world.

And if you think about it that way, that's where the fear comes from. What am I going to do without my best friend? By putting down the beer, you're voluntarily putting away your best friend. It's a very difficult thing to do. It's a very, very real fear.

• • •

There is always hope. Always hope. And you *can* do it. Anyone can do it at any time. You just have to make up your mind. The most important thing I've learned through my disability and everything else is that just because you can't see a way to do it at the time or just because it seems impossible, think about it from a different angle and you'll be able to do it.

There's nothing I can't do. I'm sitting here in a wheelchair. There's absolutely nothing I can't do and nowhere I can't go. I do it slightly differently from everybody else, but I still do it. I can fly to Ireland on a plane by myself, to the shock and horror of many people. But nevertheless, I do it. There's nothing you can't do.

It's a matter of making up your mind and figuring out a way. And when you get sober, it's just the same. The thing is not to panic and not to give up. Never give up. Be stubborn. Be pig-headed. Be obnoxious. But don't let the damn thing beat you. You're bigger than it is.

Roasted Chicken with Pumpkin and Parsnips

Dominique Tougne
Executive Chef, Bistro 110

• • •

1   large chicken, cut in quarters
2   pounds pumpkin meat, cut in cubes, 2" x 2"
4   peeled parsnips
1   large Spanish onion
4   cloves garlic
1   tablespoon fresh rosemary
1   tablespoon fresh thyme
2   cups chicken stock
2   tablespoons olive oil
   salt and pepper to taste

• • •

Peel and cut the onion in medium size chunks. Cut parsnips the same way. In a large pot, bring one tablespoon of olive oil to smoking point. Sauté onion and parsnips over medium heat for 4 minutes uncovered. Stir. Remove and set aside.

In the same pot, add one tablespoon of olive oil and sauté chicken pieces over medium heat, 3 minutes on each side, until light brown color. Add the crushed cloves of garlic, the chicken stock, the diced pumpkin, the parsnips and onions. Stir gently. Bring to boil. Salt and pepper to taste. Add thyme and rosemary. Reduce heat, cover and simmer until the chicken is cooked, about 40 minutes. Stir frequently.

If desired, serve the dish directly from the inside of a large hollowed pumpkin.

Serves 4

Dominique Tougne is a member of the board of directors for Inspiration Corporation. He has been volunteering, planning and preparing the Anniversary Dinner, Inspiration's annual fall fundraiser, for several years. Each Anniversary Dinner is a multi-course extravaganza.

"We are spoiled in the restaurant industry," he explains. "We have whatever we need and more than what we need. At Inspiration, I give what I can, and the guests give what they can to better their lives. It is a beautiful exchange."

Chapter Two

GENEROSITY

"Now I can help others."
Robert Willingham

"You don't have to look like you're homeless."
John Hart

"All people have are memories of us."
Alfred Smith

"Not gonna do what my father did."
Jose Contreras

⊰ Curried Chicken Salad ⊱
Chef Sharon Goodloe Ako

Robert Willingham

"You know me. I can't not come to the cafe," he tells me. His smile reveals two slight dimples that offset his hazel-brown eyes. His broad shoulders and solid build only accentuate his soft-spoken ways.

Robert is an alum of The Living Room Cafe. He told me once that when he had money, he could never hold onto it. It just burned through his pocket. But now that he makes fifty dollars a week working at his church, he feels his needs are met. And he wants to pass that on.

When I look back, I think about how, out of millions and millions of people, the cafe reached out to help *me*. I look at what they've done for me. I look at everything they go through just to help one person, when society tells them they're a nobody.

I think God put me there for a reason. He helped me get on the right track. There are people out there who never ever, ever hear a voice of hope. They're just wandering in the wilderness for a lifetime. So the way I look at it, I was placed at the cafe for a reason—so that now I can help others.

See, in everybody's life there's always a rainbow. But in order to find the rainbow, you got to be willing to change, to be shaped by it. I had to sit down and realize life is not just going to give me everything I want. Some things you have to work for.

And going through all of this, I realize now that God always holds out his hand. He expects us to take his hand. There is always somebody out there who wants to help. There are organizations like Inspiration Corporation.

But you're going to have to sit down and make a decision. How bad do you want it and how much will you change? What sacrifices are you willing to make in order to get the help that will allow you to be human again?

• • •

Once you become homeless, you just do what you have to do. You have no respect. No place to go. You know you exist but you have no presence. You have no…you have no…no reason to live. You're nobody, until you run across somebody who wants to reach out and help you.

One day when I was homeless—I was walking five miles, sometimes ten miles a day, going from place to place—that's when I ran across the cafe, a place where they treat you with dignity and respect. After being referred from another program to the cafe, they taught me how to hope. They taught me how to live. How to be human.

. . .

Now I feel like I have definite worth. Like I'm worth a million dollars, even though I don't see the money. I know I am worth something.

I know God has given me a reason to live. I have a purpose. In the same way God has brought many people into my life and these organizations that helped me, now I can take that same respect, that same love, and help people less fortunate than myself.

I can volunteer my time with organizations, youth groups, elderly homes. I can give back some of my time and effort and resources. I have regular housing through my church, and with all my physical and spiritual needs being met, I can give back what was freely given to me. My purpose now is to help other people get to where I'm at.

See, now there's somebody else there. There's somebody else walking in my shoes. They just want somebody to reach out to them, to hold their hands, to show them, and to really tell them that you don't have to live like this. There is a better way to live.

It's never too late to change. The thing I had to do was sit down and make a decision. Do I want to live? Do I want to die? Otherwise I'd still be lost. Lost in the economic system. Lost in a depression.

I don't want to die. I want to be something for my daughter. I mean, just something she can live by. A positive influence. When she was born, I was wishing that I was there. She's never been homeless, but I realized that if I didn't learn to live, and by the grace of God, to live how he intended, then there's no way I can teach her about living.

And now that she is three years old, I am an example for her. I don't want her to go through the things I went through. So if it comes down to making a hard decision about whether she should go to college or whether she should take this job, she'll know to sit down and weigh the options, to think about which will benefit her more.

And whatever she does, she'll have someone there when things get hard, someone who can have a positive influence. She can sit down and say, "Now Daddy, what should I do? Should I go to college? Or should I get a job?"

• • •

Now that God has blessed me to have certain things, there are things I don't even have a desire for. I'm content to have what he gives. And I'm happy because for the first time in years I found out that having financial wealth is not everything.

It's nice to have everything you ever wanted, but at some point I became content with what I have. It's like I weighed what I have and what I don't have, and now I look at my needs first and my desires second. I'm finding out that if I had known better, if I had been taught how to save money, I might not have been homeless.

And once my daughter grows up, I'm going to teach her about how to save money and what money is used for and how to spend it wisely. See, having a job making fifty dollars a week has finally taught me the value of money. It's not so much what you have, it's how you live.

Sometimes the thing I want, when I get it, I'm not satisfied because it's something I wanted. But when my needs are addressed, I'm satisfied. I mean, spiritual wealth, reaching out and helping someone else, I get more pleasure out of that than buying things. I found out people are the most important resource God ever made.

John Hart

"I'm doing good," he tells me. "I'm doing real good." Sweat trickles down his face. Soapsuds cover his hands. Breakfast plates covered with syrup and egg yolks continue to stack one on top of the other. His smile seems undeterred. I tell him this. I know I wouldn't be smiling.

"My mom, she always say, 'You have a great smile. That's the first thing people will see.' I try not to make a big thing out of it but it's nice for people to say that to me. It's nice to hear."

At thirty-five, John is tall and slender. He told me once that he can eat and eat and eat and never gain any weight. The morning of our interview he wears a fresh linen shirt the color of sand and dark shorts. His small silver-rimmed glasses match his well-groomed appearance.

I stopped at the Salvation Army. They were having a block party. I got up to get a second helping and a lady walked up to me. We started talking. She asked if I was from around here and I said, "No, I'm from Cabrini Green. I come this way to get away from there."

We sat down. Talked. Took a walk around the block and down to the park. It got late in the day. She said she'll see me tomorrow. The next day, we met up again. Went to Salvation Army. Had breakfast. Hung out a little while longer. And as the days and months went on, we established a relationship.

I started showering her with gifts and things. She cooked for me. And, she can really cook good. She showed me where the shelters were. Told me about Inspiration Cafe. Said I needed a case manager and a referral.

But I still had some old ways in me. I didn't want to do anything. Just wanted to be around her all the time. But Lynnett, she…she let me know that wasn't good. I had to get out there and do things on my own. She can give me something to eat and help me with a change of clothes, but I had to use my own resources.

So I took her advice and went around town. Started doing things on my own. A few months later, I joined Inspiration Cafe. I was staying at an overnight shelter.

They told me a lot of things. But Lynnett, she really helped me.

She speaks her mind. She doesn't back down from anyone. And if you don't like it, you just don't like it. But she'll let you know where she's coming from. And that's one of the things I like about her. After I met her, everything turned out fine. Just fine.

Maybe she's my angel, you know. She was a part of Inspiration Cafe. She stopped before she became an alum. She has an SRO.[1] It's just for her. Took her three years. I have to get out there and get things on my own. I can't depend on her.

Right now I'm working on getting an apartment through the cafe. And, I'm using other resources around town. I want to see which is best for me. I have more than one choice to make. And I'm very happy right now.

One thing Lynnett told me: "Just because you're homeless, you don't have to look like you're homeless." You see homeless people walking around, carrying all these bags. Wearing the same clothing day after day. Not bathing correctly. They lost their hope.

It don't have to be like that. There's places around town where you can take showers. Where you can wash your clothes and wait for them to dry. Or leave your bags, go take care of your business and then come back. You don't have to look like you're homeless.

Pretend to look busy. Pretend you're going to stay busy. You know how to take care of yourself. No one is going to walk up to you and say, "Here's a million dollars, do what you want to do with it." You have to do it for yourself.

And if you're looking good, it's not going to give you a name. Everyone has a name on the street. Look at him, he's a bum. He don't care. Or look at him, look like he got a job. He always dressed up. You can't tell I'm homeless because I'm always dressed up.

It makes me feel good about myself. I can walk around town, even though I'm homeless, and people say, "You looking good." That makes me want to dress up even more. Makes me want to smell good every day.

People start giving you respect. I don't want to brag on myself, but when I walk around town, I walk with my head up high. I speak to ladies and ladies speak to me. I speak to the guys and the guys speak to me. I carry on. I can't just stand still. That's what people do. They stand still and wait for things to happen. But you can't. You have to walk.

I'm walking toward a higher goal. When I came to the Uptown area, my goal was to get my life back on track. I wasn't looking for a relationship. I was looking for a better me. And I wasn't really sure which direction to go to find a better me or to be a better me.

After high school, my son was born. My mother passed. That kind of set everything in motion. I went to the hospital for mental issues. I couldn't get over my mom passing. I'd just made nineteen and she left me. I depended on my mom for everything. And when she passed, I was lost. Didn't know what to do. Didn't know where to go. My family was me and my mom.

I started hanging out with the wrong crowd. Using drugs and doing crime and things like that. It wasn't for me. I began to be a career criminal, you know. And, I be changed. I didn't like the jails. Didn't like the running from the police.

I had to change. Either they were going to change me or I had to change myself. I went to prison in 1998. Stayed there 'til '99. Everyone told me, "This is not you. No, John. Look at yourself. You look bad. This is not the person we remember."

When I was coming up, everybody looked at me as their success story. I wanted to be a fireman. I failed once in grammar school but I made it through. Did four straight years in high school. But I started gangbanging. What we called fun then, it wasn't no fun at all. We hurt these people for no reason. My mom really got on me. Tough. Tough. Tough.

I'm the only one that graduated from high school. There were thirteen of us between my mom's children and my dad's children. I'm the youngest. It was a wonderful feeling to have my mom hugging me and crying, saying, "You did it."

But all that changed. And it's because of me. Not because my mother passed. I should've been getting stronger but I became weak. I just wasn't doing the right thing. One person might call it bad luck, but it wasn't. It was a lifestyle that I chose at that time. I had to sit back and realize that this is no type of life to live.

When I got out, I felt like I was born again. Had my head on straight. I was making better judgments for myself. Got a small job. Started buying myself clothes. Just doing things the average person would do. But then I went back to the same neighborhood.

The police pulled me over. They seen I wasn't reporting to my parole officer. I stayed another sixty-one days in jail. That was the first violation. When they released me, they sent me to a homeless shelter. I told them I didn't want to stay there. They said, "If we come get you, that's another violation." I told them to come get me.

When I was released in August 2001, I still went back to the same neighborhood but I seen it wasn't turning out. It was like a broken record, it'd skip right to the same spot. Cabrini Green was like a force field. I had to get strong enough to break through the force field, to go to another place where I can work things out for myself. And the North Side, the Uptown area was the place to be. It's a good thing to change. I was heading toward self-destruction.

When I first got to the cafe, I didn't want to do anything but eat and leave. Didn't want to do no chores. Didn't see my case manager. Didn't let anyone know when I left to see my son. And I got caught in that force field again. When I came back to the cafe, they didn't let me right back in. I had to go through the process and the paperwork all over again.

But now I'm involved in everything. They said spend some time here. Volunteer. Help out with something, even if you're just picking up paper off the floor. Ask people if you can do anything for them. And that's what I've been doing. Offering a helping hand to everyone who comes through the cafe doors.

I also volunteer at the Salvation Army once or twice a week, helping to prepare and serve the food. Every third Wednesday of the month, I volunteer at the Chicago Food Depository. And I volunteer at the Weekend Center. I put up chairs. Sweep the floor. Erase the chalkboard. I just do small things.

It doesn't have to be big things. A lot of people pointed that out to me. Lynnett calls them blessings, the small things you do for other people. And it worked out, just like they said. I really want people to remember me as a good guy—you know, if you need anything you'd call John and he'd help you.

I really can't describe how good it feels. Everyone speaks to me. And they seem to smile. Before, people didn't sound too happy to be speaking to me. But now it's like I'm involved and everyone is happy for me and that's because I am happy for myself. So I assume they're happy for me too.

I like it. I like it very much. When you change your life and you hear good responses from other people—"Oh look at him. He look good. He must've changed his life"—that makes you want to change even more, to do better things for yourself.

I know I need to see my oldest son more, so he can see me and know who his father really is. He's seventeen. My other son is seven. I wasn't there for my sons like my father wasn't there for me. I'm not blaming my father for that. I hope they don't blame me for this.

It's just that at one point I thought I…I was just going to go through life doing wrong. But I turned around so much I amazed myself. Something just come over me. I don't know what it was. I just got fed up with the negative. I had to find a better me.

And now, I am a better me. But I have to get a better and better me. I have to continue to think positive, do positive, stay active, and just keep climbing toward my goal. I can actually say that I love me. I love me the way I am. And I will love me even more tomorrow.

I want to enjoy life. A good life. I want to stand on my own two feet. I never did like crowds. Crowds carry trouble. Being with Lynnett is a crowd by itself. I just want to keep climbing the ladder to success—only not just thinking about me, but thinking about others too. We all need some help along the way.

Alfred Smith

Al sits at table five. His cane rests beside his chair. Dialysis started last month and he's less than happy about it. "If I go blind," he tells me, "I don't know what I'll do." His hands tremble as he describes all that dialysis entails.

An avid stamp collector since the age of ten, Al is sixty-three. He is heavyset with a white beard. When I ask him why he wants to tell his story, he says, "It's good for me just to reminisce, to think about days gone by."

I am the son of two immigrants. Mother was one of three German sisters who immigrated to America. Her oldest sister, Louise, she emigrated around 1926. And my mother wanted to come over, see her sister and her new little baby niece. So she came over on a winter crossing of the MS Berlin. January, 1929.

She was going to just spend one year in America. But in October, the Great Depression started. And she was of the opinion that there really wasn't anything to go back to, so she may as well tough it out and stay in this country. She never was happy about staying. She found many of the ways of America very off-putting. It was a difficult adjustment all her life.

But in 1929, she worked behind the counter in a small supermarket like they had back in those days. The depression had started. The husband and wife who owned the store were of German descent and they had relatives in Canada, whom they visited quite often.

On one of their visits, they were invited to a neighbor's home, a young German man in his early thirties. And, they were just absolutely amazed that he served bread and coffee and coffee cake. There was no bakery nearby. He'd made everything himself.

So when the husband and wife returned to Chicago, they told my mother about him. And with that, a correspondence was started between the German man and my mother, the German woman. And in the depths of the depression of 1933, he came down to see her. Liked what he saw. And made her his bride.

They produced three children. I have two older sisters. One lives in Washington, the other in Missouri. They each had four children so I have five nephews and three nieces. I keep in contact with my two sisters. We write back and forth, especially the oldest one.

I was a very loving uncle and brother. Not a birthday went by that I didn't send a greeting card to the child. And being a grade school teacher, whenever I sent in my students' book club orders, I'd always order extra books so that when the birthday time came, I'd have a present of clothing and books. Seven books at Christmas. Seven books on your birthday.

My oldest sister was especially appreciative of this. Her husband was in the military and they never knew when he might be restationed. The children knew this too. Sensed it. Made it hard to develop friendships. Not that the books were a replacement, but I'm sure they made for plenty of interesting dinnertime conversations.

And my sister being a thrifty type person, she saved them. One time, she led me into her closet and there was this huge cardboard box loaded with all the books I'd given the kids over the years. She's planning on giving them to her grandchildren because she wants them to read, just as her kids learned to improve their reading skills by reading the books I sent.

I was a very concerned uncle. I'd get in my car after school and I'd go shopping. My rule of thumb was that everything I bought for the kids had to be clearance merchandise and in good taste. Nothing really tacky or dated. Just things that were worthwhile and on sale.

My second sister lived on a ranch for a time. And I'll never forget it, one day I went into Goldblatt's hoping to find some bargain, and a clerk was putting boys' jean jackets on a table. The sign said, "Ryder brand. Originally sixteen dollars. On sale for four dollars each."

Well, I bought an armload of them and the following Christmas, Jimmy, her oldest boy, came to me and said, "I'm really happy with that jacket." And I thought, "Jimmy, I thought you would be. I thought that would be the kind of jacket for a boy growing up on a ranch."

So they all have happy memories of their Uncle Al. They remember me as being very concerned and being fun. We were a very close family. I know I disappointed them greatly by never getting married. I just don't think I'd get much in the way of satisfaction from it.

• • •

My life was on a downward spiral. I'd been a grade school teacher at one school for twenty-one years. And I burned out. Couldn't do the job anymore. The principal basically knifed me, rather than assisting me.

I was pushed out of that school after an ugly meeting with the Chicago Board of Education and assigned to a minority school on the West Side. I was completely burned out. Just tired. Very, very tired.

I survived there for a year and two months, until one fine day I basically said, "The hell with it." I got in my car and never went back.

I went to the big family home that I'd inherited. Both of my parents were since deceased. And there I was rattling around in a five-bedroom home. I decided to sell it and buy a brick two-flat. Which I did. Seven blocks or so north.

Now the house that I inherited was fully paid for but it was in serious need of repairs. I didn't get much for it. But it didn't have a mortgage. I went to the brick two-flat with a mortgage. Twelve hundred dollars a month.

Everything would have worked really well if I just had some resolve and been able to go back and teach school. But I couldn't. I just plain couldn't. I took to my bed. Belly-flopped on my bed. And I kept telling myself, "You got a mortgage. You can't live off the rent money."

I soon ran through the six thousand dollars I had in savings and found myself in foreclosure. Took all my money out of the teacher's pension fund. All thirty thousand dollars. Sometimes I think I should have talked with somebody a little more before I did it, but I really felt like I had no choice.

That got me out of foreclosure. And it gave me five more months of laying on my mattress. So then the next time I was in financial trouble, there was no saving me. There was no cushion to fall back on.

I sold the place at a fifteen thousand dollar loss. Took the money that I received and moved into a little studio apartment. Lived off the money for four years, not working. Taking to my bed most of the time. Severe and profound depression.

And when I ran out of money, I started living on SSI.² I couldn't hack it financially. I was evicted. So many of my wonderful possessions were taken from me. Thrown in the garbage. Whatever.

I lived in a park for about three months. And somewhere along the line, I heard about Inspiration Cafe. I moved to this neighborhood because of it. I was living in a shelter and coming here for my meals.

After three months in a shelter, I took a room at this flophouse across the street. I lived there for seven years. The place is loaded with cockroaches and mice. And the men are very undesirable. But what are you going to do?

About a year ago, I decided I wanted to go to counseling. So I saw the social worker and she helped me get into this building where I've been ever since. In many ways it's better, but every rose has its thorns.

I don't like being supervised as much as I'm being supervised. I'm not a kid. I don't like it. I have a housing specialist come in and take a look at me. And I have to visit once a month with another social worker here. I dislike these things very much. I'm too independent to want these things. But I have no choice. So I do it.

My apartment is a studio apartment. Wall-to-wall carpeting. My own little bathroom. A little kitchenette. Nice double bed. They furnished it decently. It's a dignified, clean older building. And the rent is phenomenally cheap. I pay for it with my SSI.

So the advantages are more than what I had before. But I have nothing. No teacher's pension. Nothing. Just SSI. I graduated in June of 1962. Got accepted into the Peace Corps. I should have gone. Or joined the military. Should have done something. Had more resolve.

If I had one word to describe myself, I'd say "unassertive." I allow myself to be pushed around too much. I'm not a take-charge person. And I should be. You have to be much more aggressive in life. I'm a marshmallow. Too much of a marshmallow.

But I was one hell of a good brother to my sisters. My oldest sister told me,

"You know Al, you dressed my kids." And she's right. I don't know where I had this energy, but I'd teach and then I'd take the El downtown and I'd go shopping, shopping, shopping.

I had what I called the Christmas closet back at home and I'd just put whatever I bought in the closet. And when Christmas came, or a birthday came, I'd have nice things to give. And I always bought everything on sale.

We're here for a time. That's all I can say. We're here for a time and then we're gone. And all people have are memories of us. Hopefully good ones.

• • •

Alfred Smith died in the early morning on April 17, 2006. He is missed by many.

Jose Contreras

Skinny and spry, Jose is always on the move—painting the hallways, baking chicken for tonight's meal, carrying in my bags. He's no stranger to helping out around the cafe.

A week before we meet, Jose pulls a folded piece of paper from his wallet. "Look," he tells me. "I have the ending." Copied in his handwriting is an excerpt from a book he's reading. Jose is an avid reader of books about success—books, as he explains, that teach you, "How to change your mind, your thoughts, your being, your person."

I'm just paying back, you know. Can't say anything bad about this place. They got me a beautiful studio apartment in a nice neighborhood, east of Sheridan, right by the lake. I really love the place I'm in. I'm not paying right now, but I will be once I'm working again.

That'll make me feel a lot better. I don't like anything for free. And nothing really is for free. Everything has a price. You got to pay something back even if it's volunteering and just doing something good. That's a way of payment. I was fortunate to come across this place.

I was married for about eight years. Got divorced. Got back together for a little while. We had a beautiful little girl, Sage, who I truly love. Love her to life.

But by the end of those eight years, I started drinking heavy, using drugs, doing things I really don't do. Started stealing…stealing liquor. Wasn't taking my medication like I am now. I deal with severe depression.

There's people who've committed suicide because of severe depression. I've thought of it at points in my life when I just couldn't take it anymore. It's a terrible feeling and your head starts to hurt. I don't wish it on anybody.

My mother suffers from it and my uncle was in a mental institution for ten years because of it. But my mom's still alive, thank God. At one time she attempted suicide. I was a kid and we were taken from her, put in an adoption center, me and my little sister.

I remember that day. We were in some car crying, just like in the movies when they take children away. I remember there were nuns and rows of beds in the place we were in. My sister wasn't there—she was somewhere else with the girls, I guess. Time passed. My grandmother and my aunt took us out of there. I went through a lot as a kid.

But after all that heavy drinking and drugging, I got myself straight. I was homeless. And too afraid to drink or use drugs because your mind isn't clear and anything can happen to you in those shelters. Shelter life. It's humiliating.

It smells. People are scratching. There are bugs. It's not good, but it's better than being out in the cold. Sometimes you just have to do things you don't want to. I'd rather be in somewhere warm on the floor on a mat. You know what I mean? But then, they're always telling you what to do. Get in line for this. Get in line for that. I wasn't used to that.

I really didn't have to go through being in a shelter. My sister has a house on Staten Island and she told me I could stay in her basement. They were willing to pay my ticket. But I refused to go because of my little girl. My mother told me I could stay with her. But I said only if I could take my daughter with me—which Sage's mother wouldn't allow.

But I'm not gonna do what my father did. Didn't ever see my dad growing up. He and my mother got divorced. My mother moved to New York. I was two. I want to be a dad for my daughter. I want to be there for her. It was hard in those shelters.

But then again, you learn from everything, right?

My daughter is five years old. She's in kindergarten now. She goes to school from 8:30 a.m. to 11:00 a.m. She stays with me sometimes, at my place, until her mother picks her up at 5:00 p.m.

We go to Blockbuster, rent a few cartoons. I feed her like crazy. She loves to cook with me, but I don't let her get close to the stove. You know she doesn't even watch the cartoons. She's so busy drawing and coloring. She'll just glance at the TV. She is something else.

This summer I'm hoping I can have her for a couple of weeks. Maybe get her into a day camp around here, so I can take her and pick her up. And I'll bring her over here so you can meet her. My little Sage.

Being a father, you know, my first kid…in a way it's kind of hard because sometimes I don't know what to do. Like when I used to take her to movies and she had to use the bathroom, I mean, you never know about those bathrooms. It's a women's bathroom and all, but now she goes in and I wait for her right there and she makes sure she washes her hands.

Her mother, she's a real nice lady. Can't say nothing bad about her because she's a wonderful woman. And I do miss her. She has two other daughters who are doing great in school so I know my daughter is going to do good in school and all that.

So like I said, you have to learn from everything. Make the best of things and always look on the positive side. That's what I do now. I used to get depressed and down on myself, but now I try to look at how—how I can fix something or how I can help myself.

I've been here almost three years. Came in the door one day. Was homeless at the time. Somebody told me about it and I wanted to see what was going on. So I walked up. Met one of the staff members, Rian Wanstreet. She was really nice. Told me about Cafe Too.

I applied. Took a test and joined.[3] I was pretty good at cooking. Had a great chef trainer, Sharon Goodloe Ako. I started working again. Moved into the YMCA. Paid my own rent and everything. Then I was in the hospital. Something happened. I don't want to get into that.

But I came here to the cafe. I was going to be homeless again, and they got me housing because I couldn't go back to work and pay my rent at the YMCA. This place has really helped me. I've been fortunate to be a part of something good because there are people worse off than me. I'm blessed to be where I am. To have everything I have today.

I still make mistakes. We're human. We all do. But I learn from them, and now I know how to change things. People *can* change. You can always make things better for yourself. I truly believe that. Anybody can be homeless. You don't have to be into alcohol or drugs. Things happen.

I read a lot of books about success. I've learned more about life from reading these books than anything else. I can't get into novels anymore or anything like that. When I was younger, I read a few. But now it's like I want to learn something. These books have a lot of lessons.

• • •

An El train rattles past the window. Jose pulls out a folded piece of paper. He reads:

The best way to help me lighten my own troubles is to help lighten the troubles of others. By so doing, I gain an inner strength and faith and the ability to face things that formerly may have seemed insurmountable. This is my resolution from now on. Certainly it can be done. And I can do it.[4]

I was a selfish person at one time. But now I truly believe in helping others because you help yourself at the same time. You feel better about yourself. And if you do good, good always repays good with good. It's a law of nature.

Curried Chicken Salad

Sharon Goodloe Ako
Head Chef Trainer, Cafe Too

• • •

36	chicken breasts (4 oz)
3	tablespoons chicken stock base
1¾	quarts water
4½	cups celery, diced small
3	cups mayonnaise
1	cup plain yogurt
1	cup green onions, thinly sliced
½	cup fresh lemon juice
4½	teaspoons garlic powder
4	teaspoons salt
¼	teaspoon white pepper
4½	tablespoons sugar
2½	teaspoons paprika
2	tablespoons curry powder

• • •

In batches, place chicken breasts in a single layer in a large sauté pan. Combine water and chicken stock base and mix well. Pour mixture over chicken. Bring pan to a bare simmer, cover with foil and keep at a bare simmer for 12 minutes. Turn off heat, flip chicken breasts and let them sit in broth for 10 more minutes. Remove from broth and chill over ice.

In a large bowl combine the mayonnaise, yogurt, green onions, lemon juice, garlic powder, salt, white pepper, sugar, paprika and curry powder. Mix well and keep refrigerated until ready to mix.

Cut chicken into medium cubes and place in large bowl. Add celery and mix briefly. Add reserved mayonnaise mix and combine well. Cover and refrigerate until served.

Serves 20

• • •

When Sharon Goodloe Ako started at Cafe Too, the thought of serving Friday lunch to the public seemed out of the question. Five years later, Cafe Too is a full-service restaurant. The culinary training program she helped design now travels to other social service agencies.

Sharon loves to teach. Her most rewarding moments come at the end of the program when students tell her, "I never thought I could do this. This is my first graduation. Thank you."

Chapter Three

FORBEARANCE

"Our place."
Ms. E.B.

"I'm not a bad person."
Sidney Wright

"You can't run nothing on me."
Cecile Stone

"I was never taught to sleep on the ground."
Joann Breivogel

↬ Warm Potato Salad with Smoked Sausage and Blue Cheese ↫
Chef Ted Cizma

Ms. E.B.

Most mornings, Ms. E.B.'s order isn't particularly time-consuming: eggs scrambled soft, bacon, a piece of toast, OJ and coffee. If the cooks are running behind schedule, she'll leave without eating.

"I'm homeless by choice," she tells me. Her fist hits the table. "Two years." Then her hands relax and she presses out her jeans, retreating. "Yeah," she adds softly. "I want to tell my story. I am homeless by choice."

What caused me to be homeless was back in '98. My father-in-law passed. My husband had just got out of the penitentiary. My son was still in the penitentiary. I was staying with my in-laws, at they house. Me and my daughter.

Once he passed, everything went downhill. All the family who wasn't living there decided they wanted to move in—my husband's sisters, they children, cousins, everybody. They was taking over my mother-in-law. You know what I'm saying? She was up in age.

She didn't know anything about writing checks. My father-in-law always pay the bills. He worked two jobs. An engineer for the Board of Education and a night clerk at the post office. He'd just retired. Had a double mortgage on the house. I didn't know the house wasn't theirs. They'd been living in it since '65.

After he passed, my mother-in-law put all her bills in my sister-in-law's hands. By her being the oldest, my sister-in-law was supposed to be taking care of it. But the bills wasn't getting paid. And by early 2000, January, we lost the house.

So my mother-in-law told my husband to find her a place. Being her only son, he was the man of the house. He found an apartment. Got a one-bedroom. We put everything in storage. The front room was huge so she kept that for herself. And then she say, she got this apartment for us.

"Oh yeah," I said. "For the three of us? You gonna let us stay with you?"

"You welcome to stay here with me. You ain't got nowhere else to go. This can be for us. It'll be ours." That's what we called it. Our place.

Everything was in my husband's hands. He's like a mama's boy. And so my mother-in-law started having him to show her how to do stuff—writing checks and paying the bills. She started cooking again and everything.

But my sister-in-law start coming over to the apartment. She come to see her brother and her mother. Wasn't like she was visiting me 'cause we don't get along. I put up with her because of my mother-in-law and my husband.

Most mother-in-laws and daughter-in-laws don't have a good relationship, but me and my mother-in-law did. I took to her. She was like my mother. We was really close. Didn't argue or fight. Nothing like that. She called me her daughter. Said I was the daughter she never had. I guess because of the way her daughters were.

Things were okay 'til my sister-in-law start staying the night. Moving stuff in. She had her own apartment, but she mostly stayed with us. She went home once a month to check on things. Come to find out, she'd been evicted and we didn't even know.

She start telling my mother-in-law, my husband wasn't taking care of the bills right. But my mother-in-law, she had no complaint 'cause the bills was being paid on time. Didn't have no problem with rent. Phone bill, cable, they was paid. We had food in the house. My sister-in-law, she just wanted to badmouth my husband.

Then she brought a boyfriend. They'd never put no food into the house. But they'd always eat up what we had. I used to complain and talk about that all the time. My sister-in-law was ready to call me bitch and what not—"This is her mama's house."

And you know, her mother always had to tell her, "No, this is our house. It's not just hers or Buddy's—she called my husband Buddy—or mine. It's our house."

We started having a lot of traffic. Had to move my mother-in-law. She couldn't sleep. People was constantly going in and out. She'd wake up and somebody be sitting in the front room with her watching the TV. Stuff of hers was coming up missing.

So we moved her into the room where she could lock the door and we came out there. But then I couldn't sleep at night. I'd wake up and people'd be standing over me. I couldn't take it. My husband, he didn't like it either.

We was constantly having problems. My sister-in-law didn't want to leave. We had to call the police a couple of times. But my mother-in-law didn't want to be involved. She knew her daughter be wrong at times, but she couldn't go against her. I understand that. I did. She say, "You grown. My son grown. Ya'll can handle it. Just don't put me in it."

This was like 2001. By the beginning of 2002, it was getting hectic. My son asked me if I could start babysitting. I didn't want to bring my grandson over to the apartment. The police was always coming for something. We thought she was probably selling drugs. We was staying in the front room, so we knew wasn't nobody coming in the front. They was coming through the alley, through the back door.

I started babysitting for my son at his place. I could walk from one place to the other. Once it got cold out, I'd just come home on the weekends. And when I did, I'd find a lot of my things damaged. Destroyed. Missing. Stolen. It just kept adding up and going on…adding up and going on 'til I couldn't take it no more.

And, my husband, he couldn't just put her out. That's his sister too. He say, "She ain't got nowhere to go." That's how it was. Any time somebody in trouble in the family, they'd always come to Mom and Daddy's house. Daddy'd find them a place, pay the first month rent, and they'd take over from there. He'd done us like that a few times, too.

But I got fed up. Couldn't take it no more. I found out about the shelters and… and I moved out. I didn't really want to stay with my son and his girlfriend because her mother and her sister was there. Her sister had her five kids. My daughter-in-law had seven.

I tried, but it wasn't working out. Too many kids. The noise. We all in one apartment now. It was crowded. I can spank my grandkids, but them others didn't belong to me. And they was the ones that was always bad or I thought they was 'cause I got so fed up, I couldn't take it.

I left and came to the shelter. And when I did tell my husband about it, he wasn't for that. My sister-in-law was telling him, "Go on, let the bitch go. She don't need to be here anyway. She ain't doing shit. She ain't worth shit."

My husband, he wanted to know where I was at. I called him after he hadn't seen me for a couple of days. My son told him they hadn't seen me. My daughter, too. He thought something had happened to me. I told him, "No, I'm on the North Side in the shelter."

So he decide to come and get me. But I wouldn't leave. I told him, "Don't try and take me. I can't go back there." I see that he would try. He'd call the police every now and then. But all they'd do was just exit her out. She come back the next day.

My husband, he didn't really want to leave his mother. But by me being his wife, we'll be married—next week on the twenty-third—it'll be twenty-eight years. I can't believe he came up here to be with me. It wasn't a thing that he wanted to do, be in no shelter. Neither did I.

And we didn't want to get money from his mother or nothing like that. My mother-in-law was getting like maybe two thousand dollars a month, pensions my father-in-law had left her. But it turned out, she wasn't seeing none of that money. All she wanted was a pack of cigarettes and a pop. She thought her money ran out.

My sister-in-law took the checks to a currency exchange. We told the guy that was cashing them that if he cashed another one he was going to jail. Then she got in good with the landlord. She'd give him the whole check and he'd take out the rent and give her money as she needed. He figured he was doing them a favor. He didn't know until we start telling him.

And all my mother-in-law kept saying was she wished we hadn't left. She even asked us to move her a couple times. But she was getting old and when it came time to move, she said she couldn't leave. It was like my sister-in-law was telling her she couldn't go nowhere.

And when we'd come to visit, my sister-in-law tell us we couldn't come in. "Her mama's not here." And we knew she was 'cause my mother-in-law didn't really go nowhere. She was a homebody. Or she'd say, "You didn't call before you come. Call next time." She not letting us in because we didn't call? It was a mess. Really a mess.

My husband, he say, "Why don't you go stay with your mama and your sister?" My mother and my sisters live in Connecticut. My mother just died last year. My husband say, if I want to live there, he'd come with me just like he came with me to the shelter. But I told him, "I'm not leaving our kids here."

My mother done lived her life. She done raised me. Now I'm with my children and my grandchildren. My family is here. My children are grown. My daughter's twenty-five. My son is twenty-nine. My mother done seen them when they was little and stuff. I want to be with mines while they little.

And then my mother-in-law got really sick. Her insurance got her a hospital bed and stuff. I used to bathe her. She was scared to stand up or sit down in the tub. I'd comb her hair, change her clothes, and everything. My sister-in-law'd call and say, "Mama want to see you."

That's the only way we'd go over there. We got tired of her not letting us in. Or when she did, we'd stay an hour or two, think we was spending the night, and then she'd put us out. It be too late to get in the shelter, so we'd walk to my son's house. He'd always let us in.

But then, you know, it'd got so it was so much, I didn't want to go to my son saying that she done put us out. He always say, "Don't be going over there. Ya'll know how she is. You must like what she's putting you through."

I got tired of hearing my son say that. So if we found an abandoned building or an abandoned car, we'd sleep there. My husband be right there with me. But I couldn't sleep. I was scared somebody might come in and kill us while we sleep…. But long as I was out of the cold….

My husband, he wasn't a punk or a coward. He didn't want to leave his mother but she'd never go with us. I think maybe by her being old, she figured that they wouldn't do nothing to her. Which nobody did. We was lucky. Nobody never did hurt her.

And now my sister-in-law's having bad luck. I'm not homeless anymore. I got my own place so I don't have to worry about her putting me out. The thing of it is, we all said something bad gonna happen to her. We just didn't think it was going to be this soon. She needs a transplant. The drugs deteriorated her kidney.

But the way she treated everybody, ain't nobody stepping forward to help her. Nobody goes to visit her now or nothing. Nobody really has any remorse about it because of how she did they mother. See, like they say, you reap what you sow. She did the whole family dirty.

Me and her, we used to get in some drag-out, knockout fights. And, I can hit hard. One time I had to get her up off me, so I knocked her butt down. Do you know she stood right back up? I hit her hard enough to lay her down there on that floor.

But my husband say, she ain't feel nothing because of the drugs. I couldn't believe that. She felt it the next day 'cause she was talking about how sore she was. And by him being a man, he would just—she hit the floor, bounce or slide over there, and then get right back up. It was like she was a zombie. She didn't feel nothing.

We knew it was a problem, when my father-in-law died. He had prostate cancer. They was giving him morphine to keep him from being in pain. My sister-in-law was caught drinking his medicine. And my mother-in-law, she had lung cancer so they was giving her the same medicine. Do you know my sister-in-law drank that medicine too?

We found out the day my mother-in-law died. We couldn't wake up my sister-in-law. We was trying to let her know that her mother done died. And when we went in her room, the bottle was in the garbage can. She was high off the medicine.

Didn't nobody make me homeless. It was my choice. I got tired of taking the abuse from my sister-in-law so I left my place to come to be in the shelter. And what I do appreciate and love about it, my husband didn't stick with his family. He chose to be here with me.

He said it was a good decision for him to follow me. Said he could've been back in the penitentiary. He was about to go astray. He knew she was into the drug thing but he was ready to try and do anything to make money. Didn't care if he got in trouble or not.

But, like I told him, "She gonna reap what she sow. Just put it in God's hands."

I look at her now and she's very sick. God do not like ugly. And she's not trying to stop. She's killing herself. You know what I'm saying?

I'm glad I'm not around her. And I'm glad my husband's not around her, either. So that's it. I'm doing very well now. I am. It just took me all through a state of depression. I go see a counselor and I take medication. I'm doing a lot better now.

I put in an application for an SRO, September 2003. Took me exactly a year. But I waited on it. September 2004. I got my own. Inspiration Cafe gave me the money I needed for my deposit. So I'm doing good. And, my husband, he doing real good, too.

I'm babysitting my grandkids. The older kids go to school so I watch the two-and four-year-old. My daughter-in-law got a new job. She couldn't depend on her mother—she's into drugs too—and she didn't want to lose her job so I told her I'd help her out. They my grandkids.

And there's nothing that I want for 'cause my son, he give it to me. He know he don't have to pay me. I didn't ask for no fee. Those are my grandkids. But he still, "Mama, you need cigarettes? You want some pop? Let me take you out."

I don't like to let him know that I need anything 'cause to me it seem like I be begging. But if he ask me do I need this or want this, I say I'll take it. I'm not gonna ask him. Don't like to ask him for nothing.

And he got all them kids, too. He just got a second job. One job wasn't fixing it. He's trying. They just moved into a house. And that's something I can say, he doing better than I did. I never owned a house. We only had two children but I never owned a house. And I love him for that. They got a home. Something I always wished I had.

I moved from the projects to a two-flat apartment building when I was a teenager. Then my father bought a home, but I didn't live in that home too long because I got married. I was there maybe a couple years. So I can say I did live in a home, but not to have my own. My son, he's doing great. He's doing real good.

It mean a lot to me to let others know how I came about from beginning to end, when things started getting rough to now. I don't have to worry about that other stuff anymore. Just have to worry about my health. So I'm okay. I don't plan on going that route anymore, being homeless.

I'm a survivor. Yeah. I can say I'm a survivor.

Sidney Wright

"I know the pain," he tells me. "I've seen the pain. You need to see it." His deep brown eyes look right through me. "I want to show you around. Maybe if you see it, you'll understand it better."

In my heart, I know he's right. But I hesitate. I've never seen the South Side through the eyes of someone homeless. I suggest a disposable camera, a portable tape recorder, other ways of seeing. But Sidney is steadfast. "I know the pain. I've seen the pain. You need to see it."

I decide to take Sidney at his word. One Sunday morning after breakfast at The Living Room Cafe, we drive up and down the South Side. 35th to 91st Street, State Street to Cottage Grove. The next Sunday we do the same. We make nine stops.

They call it the Trail. You see it in the snow. They kick you out of the shelter at 7:00 in the morning. And I don't mean 7:01. You got to be out. You got nowhere to go.

Where you gonna go? Nobody want you over they house at 7:00 in the morning. So you walk outside and you see the Trail. You see the footprints in the snow and all these people with their bags. You just follow the Trail.

Every place got a different trail. The North Side. The West Side. The one on the South Side, the one I know, is like a circle going nowhere. It just loop around.

In the morning, it take you about forty-five minutes to an hour to walk to a day shelter, a rest stop, an oasis. That's all it is. You got to leave there by 2:30 p.m. to get back in line. Got to be in line no later than 3:30 p.m. They let you in about 5:00 p.m. At 8:00 p.m., they close the doors. Day in and day out. Get in that rut and you just in a routine. You ain't doing nothing.

The people around you—I stay with thieves, murderers, fags, con men, men who just got out of prison, they got no place to go, nothing to do. They put the mental people out, too. They need a place to stay. And then, it's just a bunch of men. That tension, you know. Everybody want to fight everybody. Everybody wants to be a man.

There are a lot of young ones. I think that's just a goddamn shame. Took me forty-seven years to get homeless and you twenty-something? What the hell you gonna do when you thirty? Half of them high. Half of them want to fight. You got two, three different types of gangs together. They all homeless. Then you got neutrons like me. Don't know nothing.

Everybody constantly telling you what to do. Get in this line. Get in that line. I'm so sick of lines. And, you got to do it. Just swallow that pride, you know.

• • •

We stop at a red light. I look over at Sidney in his worn trench coat and brown fedora.

"So that's what you want me to see?" I ask. "The Trail?"

"Yeah." He looks straight ahead. He directs me to our first stop, a small neighborhood church. We park across the street, next to a vacant lot.

He's an excellent preacher. The way he talks, you know, it sounds great. He's the kind of guy who'll come and get you at the shelter. Lots of preachers say where they need help, usually for demolition. That's a big job. The company work you the whole damn day. Tearing down walls. Pulling out wires. Gutting the whole building.

Thirty-five dollars. Sometimes, fifty. But you know damn well what you supposed to get paid. If you hurt, you just hurt. And they don't care about the clothes you got on. If they didn't give away clothes at the shelter the day before, you just gonna come home—I hate to call a shelter home—you gonna come back to the shelter dirty. They don't care.

I mean, a man trying to get his shit together now. I ain't got shit. Thirty-five dollars. How much did I make the day before? Nothing. They know it's people who ain't got nothing else. And it ain't just preachers now. You got lots of cheap labor in shelters. Lots of muscle.

But this here preacher, he don't pay your money right. He want part of your pay. Five, maybe ten dollars for his tithe. When you out on the street, you got to get your money. I mean, I pay my tithe because I want to, not because he makes me. I ain't trying to hurt a preacher but I ain't trying to get hurt, either. I just don't understand it. Don't piss on me and tell me it's raining. Tell me it's pee. That's what you're doing.

Now, thirty-five dollars can give you bus fare when you trying to look around for a real job. It can buy you some roll-up cigarettes. They about a dollar or two. Get you a girl. Go in one of those abandominiums. An abandoned building, we call them abandominiums. You know, get you a place to stay.

I use humor a lot. Got to. It might be warped-ass humor but, you know, it's humor. It's funny to me. Keeps me from crying. If I take everything serious, I'd be f—ed up. I've done things I'm disappointed in, but I'm not a criminal or anything. I'm not a bad person. Shit.

• • •

We drive quite a distance, about twenty or more blocks south. Our next stop is also a church. This church is much larger and has its own campus.

Sunday is a…a rough day when you out here on the street. You up at 7:00. Most people, if you have a life, work Monday through Friday. Sunday's their rest day. Ain't nobody want to hear you waking them up at 7:00. Not on a Sunday. I don't care if it's your brother, sister, mama, daddy…. Nobody want to hear you that early.

So this church comes, pick you up. Feed you breakfast. Keep you all day 'til 2:30 p.m. or so. Bible study, membership classes, sermons. In the wintertime, it's cold outside so it's a full house. I'm a believer in Jesus and I'm learning something, so it work for me. Going up and down every day, you tend to get a little religious anyway. You get a little bit closer, you know.

• • •

From here, we drive through the neighborhood where Sidney grew up, 63rd and

Vernon. Chicago-style three-flats and front stoops line the street. We park alongside a red brick house where Sidney lived before he became homeless.

I got thrown out. Lost everything. I left with what was on. Literally. The clothes on my back. It was January. January 3, 2002.

Everything I had was in there, clothes, pictures. My sisters threw it all away. What kind of shit is this? For you to be evicted, you get thirty days. They gave me a f—ing five-minute notice. That's what you think of me?

I've never been to jail. Never been no gangbanger. When I did do bad things, I stayed away. I'm smart enough to stay away. I had a good job. Drove a truck for a few years. Post office for about fourteen years. Electronics about ten. Before I was homeless, I was unemployed. All except for the last couple years, it wasn't ever hard for me to bounce back and get another job. It might not be the job I wanted, but it be a job. I always had money…money gone.

• • •

I ask, "How does it feel to be back in your old neighborhood?"

Well, it don't mean shit to me now. I don't live here no more. But growing up, it was nice. Nothing but families. Nothing but houses all around. We went to St. Ansel grammar school. My oldest brother went to De La Salle, an all-boys Catholic high school. I started out there but graduated from Mendell, a public high school. My younger brother went to Hals Franciscan [another all boys Catholic high school].

• • •

"Come on," Sidney says suddenly. "I got something to show you."
We drive to his brother's house, not more than five minutes away. I'm greeted warmly. The resemblance between the brothers is striking. I stand in the living room

and admire the painted family portrait framed over the mantle. Sidney is the middle child of five. His mom and dad are both deceased.

While the two brothers sit at the kitchen table, leafing through the Sunday paper and catching up on family news, I take in all of their father's artwork. It's everywhere. Wooden sculptures. Oil paintings. African masks.

I'm drawn to a small portrait at the bottom of the stairs. A young boy, wearing overalls, sits in a large cardboard box, hugging his knees to his chest. Sidney walks over and smiles. He used to model for his father's paintings when he was a child.

As we're walking out the door, Sidney tells his brother that I'm writing a book. He seems surprised. So I start explaining the project and how the Living Room Cafe is a part of Inspiration…. Sidney cuts me off.

I guess I'm a little proud. I don't tell my brothers and sisters. That's why he didn't know nothing about The Living Room Cafe. I don't tell them about my trials and tribulations. They know I was out there. But that's *all* they know. They can't tell you where I stay. I keep things to myself. That's what I know. That's what I do. I've always been private like that.

You can see I come from good stock. I'm a good person. I'm fairly well-educated. Never been in jail. Never been no big dope fiend or pusher or none of that other negative shit you hear. I'm not a street person. Well, I wasn't.

When I first went out there, I had nowhere to go. Reality set in and it's really f—ed up. Shit happens, you know. I was just thrust into it. I didn't know. Never been in the streets. I mean, I knew of the streets. But I've lived it the last couple of years. It's pretty hard out there on the trail.

I take two steps forward and three steps backwards. Then two steps forward and one step backward. Still, I'm getting somewhere but shit, look how slow it is. I get tired. And I'm around a bunch of guys. Everybody's telling me what to do. When to get up. When to go to sleep. How to do this. How to do that. And if I don't want to do it, there's always somebody else waiting to take my place.

I'm not the begging type. I got pride. Never let them see you sweat, you know.

Pride'll kill you. I know it's going to kill me. I don't ask for shit. If I need some money from you, I tell you I need $1.17. I don't care if you pull out a twenty and say, "Here take it."

No. I don't need your twenty. Just give me the goddamn $1.17.

Pride. I got my pride.

• • •

A week passes. Sidney and I head out again. Our next stop is an old public school that's been converted into a shelter. The area around it looks desolate. There's no one in sight.

It's open from 8:00 to 10:00 at night. You see guys lining up here about 5:30 p.m. You got to be here by 7:00 to get in. They only take about a hundred people. And after thirty days, you can't come back for six months.

You can't get your shit together in *no* thirty days. Even if you get a job right now, it's gonna be two to three weeks 'til you get your first check. And you gonna need another check, unless you making five hundred or a thousand dollars. With the minimum wage at $6.50, you can't get you a place.[1] It's gonna take you a good two months, not no thirty days.

• • •

"What's it like on the inside?" I ask.

You sleep on beds. Fifteen to twenty people in a classroom. It's real clean on the inside. You can take you a good nice long shower and they feed you halfway decent.

But the guards, they treat you like shit. Do this. Do that. In the wintertime, they can do what they want 'cause it's cold outside. What you gonna do? In the summertime, you can say f— it. Sleep outside. Walk the streets. But in the wintertime, they hard on you.

They pat you down. Make sure you got no weapons, ink pens, papers. Just like you in jail. They take your stuff—you know, our bags—and put them to the side. Someone can easily get up, say that's their bag and walk out. But that's only if you let people know what you got inside your bag.

• • •

We drive to another shelter. Sidney tells me he spent the most amount of time here, off and on for the past few years. The building looks austere and uninviting. A few tiny windows.

Doors open at 5:00. You have to be in by 6:00. The line starts like 3:30 p.m. You get in, take a shower—not a private shower, now. It's with a bunch of other men. Then they feed you. They wake you up at 6:00 and you start that cycle all over again.

I was smart. I'd always get me a letter—copy it with a header so it look official—that say Sidney works such and such and he comes in at such and such a time, you know. I got away with that shit.

To me it was humiliating 'cause this is my neighborhood. I really don't want you to see me in line. It's highly embarrassing. But after a point, I was like f— it. So you see me in line. I ain't ask you for shit. And if you do know, you not helping me. These people are.

But once you lose that embarrassment, you become more bum. I know homeless people, we can be more critical than anyone else. When you down and out, you tired of everybody telling you what to do. You're just more critical of everybody else. Me and these couple of guys, we just start categorizing people. We all homeless.

A **bum** is just a guy who's always begging. He say, "I'm gonna bum me a cigarette. Gonna bum me a transfer."

A **tramp**, he on the trail. He going from this place to that place, wherever the food at or the clothes give away. It's a trail and he just trample on it.

A **hobo**, he travels. He don't be around all the time. He go to Gary, Indiana. The Salvation Army in Joliet. He get away for a couple of weeks, probably 'cause somebody after his ass. Usually. And then he come back.

A **derelict**, he just out there. He give up, like the people who live under the bridge. Their mind's messed up in some kind of way. They just give up trying.

Me? I'm a paycheck away from being on the trail. Just a regular guy. A tramp. It ain't like I'm really up. All I did is get this apartment through the cafe. Not like I'm really the man again.

• • •

I kept me a weapon. The people there scared the f— out of me. Nobody give a f— about you. You gonna get robbed. Somebody always gonna try to fight you. Don't they know, ain't no man scared of no other man. I ain't got to box you, but when you turn your back….

I know my rages. I got nothing to lose. When you stuck in these situations and you feel that hopelessness, you really a dangerous person. I didn't give a f—. Didn't care about nothing. Nobody. If you ain't for me, you against me. You know.

I almost did things I shouldn't have did. You got hustlers, male prostitutes, rapists, cut-throats out here. One guy was out on the West Side staging accidents. All these tramps kept showing up in the shelters with broken arms. He'd put a board on your arm, both sides, take a hammer and break your arm. Get you more money for your injury.

I ain't no hustler, but those kind of demons get to you. Made me think, "You know I do need some money." I never went for it, but it made me say, "Hmm."

Think about that. I only been out here a couple of years. Just think of people, that's all they know. Once you start saying, "I ain't got nothing to lose," you the most dangerous person in the world.

It aged me about seven or eight years. I didn't used to have all this gray and baldness and bad attitudes. You know, just not caring. It's in my heart to care. I'm not trying to live that kind of life. But things happen to you. I had money. Lost it. I'm just trying to get back. Trying to do better. Got me a phone now. So I'm getting back into the circle. Back into society.

• • •

We start driving again. We go north to a day shelter, a resting place on the Trail. We drive through block after block of scattered homes, abandoned buildings and vacant lots. A handful of people are out and about. In the distance, an abandoned elevated train line runs parallel with the street.

Every day you walk. This is your walk. Back and forth. You walk by yourself. There's always safety in numbers but you see the same people every day. They talking about the same old shit. I'm tired of that. But what you gonna do? I ain't got shit to do all day. It's like day shelter, overnight shelter. Day shelter, overnight shelter. That's what you do every day.

Rain, snow, sleet, I don't care. You out the door at seven o'clock. And you gonna get wet. You don't have an umbrella. Who gonna keep an umbrella?

The day shelter supposed to help you get an apartment or a job. They feed you breakfast and lunch. You can take a private shower. Get clothes. Pick up your mail. If you looking for a job, you can give them their number. That helps. I mean, they help you the first week or so. Once they get to know you, you just another number. Or so it seems.

• • •

We leave there and I drive Sidney home. We drive through all kinds of neighborhoods, from famous South Side mansions to worn down public housing, from boarded-up buildings to newly gentrified homes. I ask Sidney what it means for him to tell his story.

Someone could have told me and I wouldn't have had to go through this shit. F— experience being a teacher. I'd rather read about times being hard. I wouldn't wish this on my enemy. It's just terrible. Hopefully, someone won't have to go through this. You don't deserve this shit.

Cecile Stone

You don't often find Cecile by herself. Taylor and Tevin are always somewhere out and about. They travel together. A threesome. Taylor is seven and Tevin is four. Taylor is always on the go, seeking attention, talking to everyone she meets. Tevin tries to follow his sister's every move, but he is quiet. He watches you, drinks you in with his big brown eyes.

"My real name is Celina," she says softly. "It means 'little heaven' in Spanish. My grandmother named me."

Her smile is warm but short-lived. Cecile is thirty years old. Her frame is slight, her fingers thin, her cheekbones sharp against her sunken cheeks. She has on her favorite outfit, a pair of comfortable navy blue sweatpants.

"I'm a survivor," she tells me. "I've been out on these streets for years. You can't run nothing on me."

Weaving her words into a poem was my choice.

I.

I want to let everyone know the roughness in life.
The trials and tribulations you go through to succeed.
I've had a pretty rough life.
My mother died when I was fourteen.
My father verbally abused me.
I've always been "a f— -up."

> "You won't amount to shit.
> You're not going to be nothing in life."

Tried to commit suicide after my mother died.
> Got sick of my daddy.
> I tried everything.

I done tried suffocating myself.

I done overdosed on pills.
I done tried slitting my wrists.
I done did everything.
At fourteen.

If I'd had a gun in my hand, I'd be dead.
I'm glad I didn't get no gun.

II.
I been kicked out of the house.
    Been living in shelters.
    Been through a lot of stuff.

My mother wanted to stay alive long enough to see me succeed in life.
That's what keeps me going.

I got pregnant with my daughter in January of '97.
I was twenty-two.
It was rough.
I was back staying with my dad.
"You should give her up.
You're not going to get your life together."

"F— it. I can't do it no more."
I came to Chicago.

In 2000, I was staying in a shelter.
Ended up getting pregnant with my son.
Had to swallow my pride to put my kids in a shelter.
It was just horrible.
It's twice as rough with children.

I been working funky little jobs, here and there.
    Used to work at Wrigley Field.
    Used to work at Soldier Field.

Used to work at Factory Card Outlet.

This year is the year for me to bust my butt and get a house for me and my kids.

I just done a lot of bad.
I done did a lot of bad choices.
There's been times when I sit back and think,
"Oh man, I did this."
I start crying.
My daughter start crying.
My son, he just stare at us.

I done did a lot of ignorant crap.
Ignorant.
Both my kids, they daddy's not in they life.

My son, he's a bully.
I used to be just like my son.
I'm the littlest between me and my brother.
I'd always be fighting his battles.
My roommate's kids, they fight a lot with my kids.
I told Tevin, "If they hit you, you lay they ass out."
He be trying to do it too.

Taylor, she try to be Mommy.
"Tevin get over here."
She be yelling at Tevin like she the mommy.

III.
I'm dating a young boy.
People say, "You can't love him."
But I do.
He just need to grow up.

He got 'til the end of January to do exactly what I put in the letter.
I gave him an ultimatum.
Maybe once that kick in, he'll change.

Been raped twice when I was younger.
Been in two abusive relationships.
Ain't no love in the world if a man put they hand on you.
And they not going to talk downwards to me like my father.

My boyfriend, he call me stupid.
I get on him a lot when he do.
"How you gonna call me stupid?
I got a high school diploma.
I got two kids.
I got twelve years on you.

Twelve."

He eighteen.
I'm thirty.
He act ignorant sometimes.
He just young, so he immature.

These guys out here, they think they can run the script on the female.

Right.

I done heard it all.

"You really think you running something past me?
The only reason why you do is 'cause I'm letting you do it.
    You stay in my house.
        Smoke my cigarettes.
           Eat my food….
    You too young."

Please! I know.

I been out on these streets thirty years.
I know.

IV.

If my mom was alive,
I wouldn't be going through none of this.
I wouldn't had dropped out of school.
I wouldn't had no kids.
And if I did, they daddy's would be living in the house.
My mama didn't play that.

V.

I go to a counselor.
I go to talk to her, not like crazy or anything.
    I just need someone that I can actually talk to.
It's hard carrying all this around in me.
I got like thirty ulcers sitting in my stomach.
I got a four hundred pound monkey on my back.
        Stress.
        My boyfriend.
        Losing my apartment.
        Trying to find a job.
        Trying to get my kids a good life.

I don't go to church.
Only thing I do is pray.

I'm gonna make it on my own.
Forget trying.

I'm gonna make it on my own.

Joann Breivogel

Her black crocheted hat is pulled down over her forehead. She wears several layers of clothing despite the late summer heat. Three plastic grocery bags overflowing with papers, torn envelopes and newspaper articles rest beside her chair. She is a petite woman; her thin fingers pick at her breakfast.

At present, Joann is barred from the shelter. Her children are grown. They were raised by family and now live in Florida. Her second husband died in 2002. Her first husband died when she was twenty-five.

Mine's kind of a quiet story. I live a quiet life. I do usual everyday things like other people do, go out to look for a job and hope that eventually I'll get the job. A full-time job. Not a part-time job because part-time doesn't pay much for an apartment. You want an apartment that's gonna make you feel better about yourself and help you get your life together. Have better luck. Seems to me, my luck has always been lost. Not been found.

Right now I'm having a lot of problems with the shelter coordinator. I live in the streets. I can't tell you whether I'm scared or not—I just don't like walking the streets at night. I should be getting my sleep. I stay awake all night. I don't choose to sleep on the ground. I was never taught to sleep on the ground. Nothing like that. You sleep on a bed, not on the ground.

Sometimes I get to the shelter late and sometimes I get there quite early, but most of the time, I don't get the chance to go over to the women's center every evening at 4:30 p.m. to sign up. So they keep kicking me out, and kicking me out, and kicking me out. I cursed out one of the women in there and the security guard.

That's how I wound up getting barred and having to go see one of the coordinators. I got angry because it's been quite often. I didn't like what was happening to me. Seems to me like I'm just somebody to pick on and I don't see myself as somebody being picked on. Hopefully, I'll get back in.

The shelter coordinator is kind of difficult to talk to. They act like they don't want to talk to you at all. Like there's something holding them back from talking to you. So I'm going to run for office. People not doing what they're supposed to be doing and you feel really bad about it and you want to do something about it.

I go to the doctor every month. I take my medication. We sit down and we talk about the same thing we talked about before, about what I'm supposed to accomplish and how I feel about where my life has taken me and what I'm doing with my life. I never thought of myself as being homeless until I became homeless.

Growing up, I always wanted to be an airline stewardess. My second choice was to work in housekeeping in a big beautiful hotel. My life's not really together the way I want it to be, the way I want to be able to react to situations. There's a lot of stuff I still want to do and I'm not doing it yet. I think I lost a lot of time being the way I am, so quiet.

This is hard to do, to talk about your life and what happened in your life and how many people you knew back in your lifetime, how many jobs you had, how many places you been, how many places you want to see…and all the things that I didn't do that I should have done.

I would've had a profession. I would've had money. I wouldn't have to stay in somebody else's place, waiting for somebody else's food. You don't feel comfortable about it. It's not your food and somebody else is feeding you. You're not feeding you.

Like, you go to work and you work a full day, and you go home and you can fix your own food because you went to the store and you bought it. Here, it's not too hard to deal with, but it's still somebody else's food. They went to the store. They buy it. They fix it for you. I want to feed myself.

· · ·

You haven't asked me a lot of stuff. What's your favorite vegetable? What's your favorite candy bar? What's your favorite movie? What television show you like to see?

"All right, let's do it. What's your favorite movie?"
I like movies that star Marilyn Monroe. Shirley Temple. Grace Kelly. Old time

movies. Lucille Ball and *I Love Lucy*. A lot of those shows I grew up on.

"What's your favorite candy?"
Starburst.

"And your favorite TV show?"
Star Trek. I like science-fiction shows. They talk about the stars and about the universe.

"Your favorite food?"
Pork chops. I love pork chops. Hamburger too, but let's say pork chops. And in the morning, like people who have to have their daily coffee, I like to have a daily juice.

There's one more thing I want to add. I want to say that being homeless and not being in an apartment is really tough on you. I don't like the homeless thing. I don't like it at all. You're out there on the street trying to stay up all night long. You got no money and you can't go no place else. It's not like you can go someplace and get you a cup of coffee and sit down and relax. It's not like that. I hope I never have to be homeless again. That's what I want to say.

• • •

Six months later, at the fourth annual cafe talent show—a tradition she start-ed—Joann leans into the microphone. Her black crocheted hat, pulled down over her forehead, hides her eyes but not her smile. Her voice, soft and raspy at first, grows more confident with each chorus:

> "Reach out and touch somebody's hand,
> Make this world a better place, if you can."[2]

Warm Potato Salad with Smoked Sausage and Blue Cheese

Ted Cizma

Executive Chef, John G. Shedd Aquarium

• • •

1½ pounds small Yukon Gold potatoes, sliced ¼ inch thick

¼ cup plus 1 tablespoon extra virgin olive oil

    salt and freshly ground pepper

2 cooked smoked sausages,

    such as andouille, about 3 ounces each

1½ tablespoons red wine vinegar

1 tablespoon minced shallot

2 teaspoons Dijon mustard

1 small bunch arugula, trimmed

1 green onion, white and tender part only, thinly sliced

¼ pound blue cheese, crumbled (½ cup)

• • •

Preheat oven to 400 degrees. Position a rack in the upper third. On a large rimmed baking sheet, toss the potatoes with 1 tablespoon of olive oil and season with salt and pepper. Spread the potatoes in a single layer and roast for 12 minutes, turning once, until barely cooked. Add the sausages and roast for about 10 minutes longer, turning them once, until the potatoes are tender and the sausages are lightly browned and heated through. Blot the potatoes and sausages dry with paper towels and cut the sausages into ⅓ inch thick slices. Transfer to a large bowl.

Meanwhile, in a small bowl, whisk the vinegar, shallot and mustard. Slowly whisk in the remaining ¼ cup of olive oil and season with salt and pepper. In a medium bowl, toss the arugula with 1 tablespoon of the dressing and a pinch each of salt and pepper. Transfer to a platter. Add the rest of the dressing to the potatoes and sausages, then toss in the scallion. Add the blue cheese and toss quickly. Mound the potato salad over the arugula and serve.

Serves 4

· · ·

Ted Cizma prepared the second Anniversary Dinner extravaganza in 2000. Living up the street from Inspiration gave Ted a real sense of connection to the cafe. He believes "the simple act of preparing food connects us all on the most basic level, giving us common ground."

A native of Chicago as well as a former dockworker and self-taught chef, Ted was named one of Food & Wine *magazine's choices for the best new chef in 2000.*

Chapter Four

⇥ HUMILTY ⇤

"You never know who you're going to be with."
Shiriony Shrodney VanChilds

"We're all connected."
Rian Wanstreet

"Never kick a person when they're down."
J.C. James

"This is where I wanted to be."
Michael Mudd

⇥ Zucchine A Scapece ⇤
Jonathon Goldsmith

Shiriony Shrodney VanChilds

Named for his grandparents, Shirley and Rodney, Shiriony sat at table two. He looked tired. His skin was ashen. A thin blue canvas messenger bag rested beside his chair. I joined him for breakfast and discovered that it was his first morning at the cafe. He'd been on the waiting list for a year and a half.

Nine months later, we sit in the basement of the Weekend Center. His studio apartment is on the second floor. This morning, his bag carries three books of inspirational sayings, several school applications, and two small paintings that were given to him.

On the floor beside him is a floral arrangement he created years ago, one that started in a tin can with two fabric roses, some twigs, and a black raven's feather. Shiriony's voice is low and deep as he describes their symbolic meanings. His skin is radiant. His eyes dance.

He reaches for one of his books and reads aloud. His voice booms, and then all at once decrescendos. Weaving his favorite sayings into the fabric of his story was a decision we made together.

O ne night, I was on the train. It was like eight o'clock and this woman—she was like a jazz singer—she looked at me and said, "Boy, you're getting off this train tonight."

I looked at her. "No, I'm not. Not here. I don't know nothing about this end of town."

She said, "Yes you are. Come on."

I thought she was going to take me to get something to eat because she'd done that before, bought me breakfast. Her name was Vicki. Vicki Lester. There'd been a few people that were homeless—didn't look like they had a dime—but they bought me breakfast, dinner, stuff.

I'd been evicted. I knew *nothing* about shelters. I didn't know where to go. For six weeks, I rode the train. Didn't tell anybody. I'd get off when I saw people that knew me or I'd make up some story. I was so ashamed. So much hurt and regret.

Sometimes I'd get off the train and go over to Rose's house because she's a very good friend. But then I'd get back on the train. I told her I was staying with another friend. The friend was the Chicago Transit Authority. The whole city.

That night, Vicki and I got off the train and as we were coming up the street, we actually passed the cafe. She said to me, "I'm going to take you someplace where you can get some rest. You can't sleep on the train and then just walk around all day. You got to lay down. The body needs to be stretched out. You're starting to look like an old homeless man."

I said, "I ain't been homeless just a month."

But she went right on. She brought me here. At that time it was an overnight shelter. And what's ironic is that I slept right there. Right there. On a mat on the floor. That very spot in the very building where I'm telling the story now.[1]

I remember that night. I just kept thinking, who are all these ugly people around me? I was just going off, you know. Vicki, she gave me her bracelet. It had rhinestones and fake diamonds. She said, "You keep this on to protect you."

She was a trip. She wore a mink coat and always kept herself together. We all knew she was crazy. I used to see her downtown when I was going to work some days. She panhandled. But, you never know who you're going to be with.

That was one thing my mother used to always tell me. Be careful about what you say because you never know which words you may have to eat. It never made any sense until I became homeless. And then I started reflecting and thinking about all the things I said about homeless people. Starting in 2001, I've had the opportunity to apologize to a lot of people and tell them that yes, now I'm homeless, too.

• • •

"We learn wisdom from failure much more than from success;
we often discover what will do, by finding out what will not do;
and probably he who never made a mistake, never made a discovery."

– Samuel Smiles

• • •

To lose someone you're close to can kill you with the hurt, the regret, the grief. That gamut of emotions, you know. Some people are never the same after someone dies. They're a changed individual. And see, from that, I overcame. Took a long time. Ten years.

I'm a Buddhist and my mother, she was a Buddhist. When she passed in 1992 that was the onslaught of a new existence for me. I never recognized it—even though my brother and sister, they knew what was going on. My mom and I, we were like this.

She was my very, very best friend. We did everything together. We'd meet sometimes after our work and go places, go shopping. Everyone that knew me, knew her. My friends would just laugh, "Is your mama coming?"

My thirty-fifth birthday was the first birthday I didn't have a German chocolate cake. I was so spoiled. I had everything I wanted. I didn't realize that I never really lived in the space of reality. I was sheltered. Still living in the same apartment that I grew up in. Totally unaware, until this one person left this earth.

I mean, I never saved money. I'd always come home with a Marshall Field's bag. I'm definitely a right-now baby. I had the money. The car. The "this." I had all these things which really meant nothing. And then I started gambling, started drinking.…

I tried to commit suicide. Sleeping pills. I didn't have any money. I was four months behind in rent. Off-site betting and the boat. I was working in Marshall Field's, the Walnut Room. I made good money. Got great tips. But I'd just go and blow it.

I wasn't even thinking about the rent. And I was afraid to go and seek help. So I suffered more. That three-bedroom apartment, I'm telling you, clothes were everywhere. I didn't care. I was totally depressed. I had good friends. They'd come by but I'd never let them in.

I never knew my strongest bond existed until it wasn't there. I took it for grant-ed. Lived like life was always going to be there. Hell, I was almost thirty-nine before I finally had the courage to see me, not the illusion. I'm the one who tried to commit suicide. Not somebody else. I did that.

And my own feeling is that—and I've talked to a lot of people about being homeless—many people took for granted the relationships they had. And so a lot of people are homeless not as a consequence of their inabilities to be stable, but because of that hurt. They're just walking around in deep shame and regret for things they've done.

• • •

You must understand the whole of life,
not just one little part of it.
That is why you must read,
that is why you must look at the skies,
that is why you must sing and dance,
and write poems, and suffer and understand,
for all of that is life.

– Krishnanurti[2]

• • •

In Buddhism, we have a chant—I chant *nam-myoho-renge-kyo* every day. The words mean "devotion to the mystic law of cause and effect through sound." It's like everything we do, we're making a cause in our life. And as a consequence, we're going to receive an effect. We're the ones that bring things into fruition.

I believe that I created the cause to be homeless because of how I used to talk about homeless people. Like a dog. They would never come and ask me for *anything*. I'd look at them and say, "Ick." To do that was *nothing*.

And that's a cause. So eventually an effect will come around. And for me, that effect was being homeless, having to go through the same suffering—wearing the same pair of pants day after day for a year, washing them only once a week.

The thing is you never know what a person's going through or why they're in the situation if you don't talk to them. You just make assumptions. So life says, okay, you're going to get one to deal with for yourself.

I've been in some dire situations since 2001 but it's been a wonderful journey. I've had to walk that same walk—and you *can* walk it. And you *can* come out even better than before. I don't think I'm better yet, but I now know how to appreciate, to genuinely show gratitude for the little things, like "Good morning" and "Thank you" and "Would you like?"

It's the inconspicuous things that sustain us. When you're staying in a shelter, they don't ask you, "Would you like the lights on?" Lights out at ten o'clock. You have nothing. No food, no extra clothing, nothing. I don't care about things anymore. They don't make a difference. What makes a difference now are people and how I impact them.

Homelessness has been a very vivid and clear look at the mirror of my arrogance. I wanted to do everything my way. Many people said that to me years before it happened. What are you doing? Why are you doing it like this? What happened to your money? Why didn't you pay your rent? Why, why, why, why?

And, I didn't feel that anyone deserved an answer. So that pushed me deeper into my own little world of thinking. I started shutting people out, slowly, all because I didn't want to say, "You're right." So I had to eat those words. I was too arrogant to get my unemployment, to get my food stamps. I didn't have to suffer. I chose to suffer.

And the more that I went through my process of reflecting on my own behavior, for my own behalf, I started to see how I wasn't taking responsibility for my own existence. I had placed my whole entire existence on the backs of my family and my friends. How arrogant is that?

Being homeless, I've had the opportunity and plenty of time to look at my life. Why I couldn't find a job. Why I'd lost every job I'd ever had. Why? Why? I could go through a list of whys about my life. But the most important one is, "Why I want to live." I finally saw how people felt about me.

Two years ago, my niece told me, "You shouldn't have disappeared just because you were homeless." My brother scolded me. He was livid. My sister-in-law, same thing. My friends were like, "How dare you disappear. We thought you were dead.

You tried to commit suicide once before so we thought you finally decided to succeed."

And I just related the whole thing to when my mother died, how I felt those feelings of loss and loneliness and emptiness. That's the same thing all of my friends and family felt when I got evicted and disappeared.

So it's just arrogance—the trips I took other people through because I didn't want to face up to the responsibility of taking care of myself. I'm not proud of that. But I have been able to find out what I really like and what I don't like about myself, and that I really want to contribute to the happiness of other people.

Now I chant so I can find wisdom. See, for so many years I used to chant for cars, for clothes, for apartments, for people, for money to buy alcohol or go gambling. But the most important thing about life is the wisdom not to suffer. The wisdom to enjoy living.

· · ·

First comes the thought,
then the organization of that thought into ideas and plans,
and the transformation of those plans into reality.
The beginning, as you will observe, is in your imagination.

– *Winston Churchill*

· · ·

I was on the waiting list for a year and a half. I'd heard about the cafe and I went there a couple times with friends but I could never get in. And I wanted in. I'd ask my case manager at Salvation Army about the cafe every day. One day, she said, "They finally called."

It was November 2004. But, I never thought I'd be housed by the cafe. That was an inconspicuous benefit. So when I moved in, April 1, I said to myself, "Now that I'm in housing, I will be employed within 120 days." I started work June 9.

It's our choice. The cafe definitely provides the tools but even they don't know how it's going to work for each individual. Some people say they are willing to take the necessary steps to end the cycle of homelessness, but those steps can get so steep sometimes.

Everyone told me I wouldn't get a grant. Even the cafe. But Barbara—she's an alum—she did research on the computer for me and as a benefit of completing the Employment Project, I have an application here for a five thousand dollar grant through the city of Chicago.[3]

Barbara found two schools, accredited programs, where I can get a degree in floral management, horticulture and ornamental design. So I'll be able to put those letters behind my name. That's still my ultimate goal, to be a flower shop owner. Black Orchid Flowers, Gifts and Scents. I even have this vision for those two huge windows upstairs. Flower boxes, shelves, hanging vines....

Right now my job is part janitor, part doorman, messenger and landscaper. And for the first time in my life, I've gained trust and credibility in the universe. I've been trusted with a job to be responsible to take care of other people. That's a privilege and an honor.

And I think it's because of housing. If you have a comfortable place to live, you're capable of creating remarkable things. But being homeless, you don't have a space where you can create anything. I tried to do flowers in the park, but you can only do so many arrangements before people look at you like you're insane, selling flowers for food.

So not only did I get the job—haven't even been there sixty days—I got promoted and asked to do more event planning. It's grace. Things just get better and better when you have support. Now I'm able to pay people back. Buy somebody lunch when they don't expect it.

• • •

There is only one thing in the world which is worth
dedicating all your life. This is creating more love among
people and destroying the barriers that exist between them.

– Leo Tolstoy[4]

. . .

I've been fortunate. Because of chanting, I know that wellspring of hope always exists in the depths of my life. If you lose that hope, you've given up the fight. I don't care what you try and do. If there's no hope, there will be *no* fight.

Now I feel like I have the ability to help people find their place. That's my commitment to ending homelessness. 'Cause if you have someone around you who is encouraging you, you can break through this shit. Like *that*.

You just need someone who knows how to motivate you and helps you to see your real authentic self. Once you do that, then you can begin to make movement that you've never made before in your life.

I'm going to build my own floral business. I'm determined. Because it's just a dream. Our lives are just a dream. And it's as great as we want it and as devastating as it needs to be in order for us to bring forth our greatness. We're the only ones who can do it.

Rian Wanstreet

I sit with Rian in her sparse new office. She sits cross-legged on a donated blue office chair. Her high heel pumps surprise me. Today is her twenty-fifth birthday; she opens a handful of cards from guests and alumni. A few tears seem to teeter on the edge, but she composes herself and straightens her slacks.

Rian came to Inspiration Cafe as an Americorps*VISTA volunteer and stayed on staff for four years.[5] Her work has included Cafe Too, Art for All, volunteer coordination, as well as community advocacy and policy work. I ask her the same question I ask everyone: What does it mean to tell your story?

I love that question. This place is all about the exchange of stories. It's one of the things that makes it so special here. Inspiration breaks down the barriers we put up between different kinds of people. Once you learn someone's history, it's a lot harder to be distant from them.

When you first come, sitting in the cafe for breakfast or dinner, it's very intimidating. I was twenty-one. Fresh out of college. I'd been exposed to a lot of different things in my life, but I was being thrown into an environment that was pretty alien. That awkwardness didn't start to pass until I sat down and started talking.

When you exchange a story, it's just remarkable. You realize, very quickly, how much everybody has in common. Regardless of their past, everybody goes through the same emotional turmoil. The full gamut of human emotions is present in everyone. It's just how it's manifested that's different.

I do a lot of work with the community and whenever I've gone to legislators or to the business community, people immediately throw up barriers when you talk about homelessness. It's faceless. Until you put a story to a face, it doesn't mean anything.

• • •

Cultivating the relationship between the police and the homeless is what I'm most proud of. I don't want to say volatile, but it's not very nice. There's a lot of distrust and fear among the clients about the cops and the cops are being told they need to get these people out of here. It's on both sides. Clients don't see past the uniform. Cops don't see past the bags.

So we organized to have the beat cops come in and serve breakfast. The first cops came in flak jackets and bulletproof vests. That's the mindset they have about who they're coming to visit. They left saying, "This is really nice. We obviously don't need bulletproof vests." The next group came in plainclothes.

We've had the sergeants from both beats and the commander of our district serve dinner. And I just think that's really very cool. It was heartening to see. They trust us now. We've had some clients who've had run-ins, but now when the cops hear you're with Inspiration, they're less antagonistic.

We really push that whole dignity and respect thing, like getting the beat cops exposed to the "Ten Year Plan to End Homelessness."[6] They had no idea about it. And it's like, why isn't that information being communicated? Why is it up to a small social service agency to tell you guys about this? But that's what I do. It's one of the things I'm definitely most proud of.

Jonit Bookheim [Housing Specialist] and I also go to every Chicago Alternative Policing Strategy [CAPS] meeting in this neighborhood.[7] We wanted to establish a large presence as a respected and well-run organization. A lot of the people who come to CAPS meetings have very set ideas about homelessness. Our goal was to try and combat that a little bit.

Like when people say things that are blatantly untrue about homelessness. Or you hear them say they saw a guy with a bag full of clothes and they took it and threw it away. It's like, "You just threw away that person's whole life. Do you not get that? That bag is that person's whole life." I mean, where does that disconnect come in? We have a house full of stuff. They have one bag.

I remember once they talked about this guy who'd ask for change. They're like, "He's obviously so high." And as they're talking I realized I knew him. He sits in front of whatever restaurant he wants to eat at that day and asks people coming by. He's not homeless. He lives at a residential home for the mentally ill. The problem is he doesn't want to eat the food there.

But people automatically assume because he talks weird, he must be high and he must be an addict. He doesn't have any teeth. He's harmless. He just wants you to buy him some food. And if you say, "No," it's not a big deal. He's never threatened anyone. I know him. I've seen him for four years now. And if I don't see him for a good period of time, I start to worry.

It's really unfortunate. There's a lot of blatant racism prevalent in CAPS meetings. But people cloud it in other issues. They're careful not to use any racial triggers. But it's about homelessness and it's about race, a lot. I mean, it's very deceptive.

And to a large extent, I don't think they know they're being racist. Racism is a much more subtle thing than it used to be. I came up here with my own prejudices that I had no idea I had until I was faced with them. I wasn't raised that way. But you grow up all your life and hear about these young black males on the news and when I walked down the street everyone looked like me, and then a young black male crossed my path and I tensed up.

What was up with that? Why did I do that? It was an instinctive reaction. Not something I could control but something I was ashamed of. A societal thing. Completely ingrained. It wasn't my fault. Wasn't my parents' fault. They didn't teach that to me. And it's not those people's fault at the CAPS meeting. I don't think they even know they're doing it. Which makes it kind of more tragic.

That's why diversity is so important. All those little interactions with people are what move us past that. It's about creating a sense of normalcy. I don't tense up anymore. But it took me four years. How long does it take an entire society?

• • •

Uptown is a very interesting neighborhood. It's very contentious and yet it amazes me. I've been really happy here. I never realized how much things could be moved until I got here.

When I was the Americorps*VISTA coordinator, I'd immediately throw out anybody's application that said they wanted to change the world. I'm glad you have that kind of idealism but you're not going to change the world. If you want to change yourself, that's the kind of application I was looking for.

But now I've seen changes made. I've gotten bills passed. I've lobbied for things.

It's much more malleable than I ever thought. What a great thing to see. People can change. You, as an individual, can make changes on a much larger scale. That's really inspiring.

I just love that about Inspiration. We give people the opportunity to focus that energy and see how they can affect a larger group. Just the alumni presence in the cafe is very impactful. To be able to see, on a constant basis, people who have been in the same situation as you. The alumni aren't perfect. People fall. There are so many cycles. But they're still here. It's just a source of inspiration. It's a very appropriate name.

I came up here knowing that I would be very changed. I had no idea how. I was going to be here for a year and then I was going to graduate school and it wasn't going to be in public policy. Now, four years later, I'm fighting very much to stay involved with the government.

I'm fascinated by Chicago's political history, its inner workings, how it moves and how you can make it move. A lot of organizations that I work with are very antagonistic. I'm not like that.

I know there are people who are truly out for themselves, but I believe people generally, given the opportunity and given the right avenue, want to help other people. But you have so many people approaching each other in such bad ways. Some groups are so in your face. When I told them I wanted to do some research and I wanted to try and talk with people, I was told merit-based organizing doesn't work. That's appalling.

We had a meeting with a realtors' association. Everyone at the national level talks about the need for affordable housing. They know what's going on. But on a local level, they're completely resistant.

So I told them, "I really respect that you guys have to make money. So how can you make money and how can you give us some affordable housing. How can this work out?"

But some groups were like, "How could you ask that? You just need to demand it."

You don't have to demand it. They're business people. We can figure out a way to make everyone happy, if you just stop yelling at each other long enough to talk about it. It's very frustrating. I feel like the entire country is like that. We've got all these red states. Blue states. Liberals. Conservatives. Nobody's listening to each other.

I know this gentleman, he's a big developer. When I met him, he was completely against affordable housing, completely against Section Eight people. Very, very scared. And rightly so. Many housing projects have been so poorly managed and there's a lot of problems with the way welfare works. That's a fair fear. Historically.

I got him involved at the cafe. He's seen how we do things. He's met a lot of people. Now he actually knows people who have Section Eight housing and he is much more amiable. He's talked to his developer friends and he's gotten a whole host of people to agree to house our clients if we want to go up into the community where he builds.

Once you know somebody's story it becomes a whole different thing. Once you put a face to a story, it's harder to be like, "Oh, those Section Eight people." You know them. You know they're into Cubs baseball and they like the same players you do. Those kind of little connections are huge.

And it's too bad they're overlooked. If you don't know somebody's story, they can be stereotyped. It's amazing what happens when you sit people down and get them to talk. It's slower. And it's harder. That's what usually frustrates people because they don't see it moving, and I do. It's just on an individual by individual basis. One person can set off a chain reaction.

· · ·

When I first came to the cafe, I got the most respect for doing something no one expected. We'd gotten movie passes. I was the Art for All coordinator. So I set it up and we went on Saturday. Only the passes were for Monday through Thursday, and I had like fifteen people with me. I paid for it. I didn't have any money, but I bought all the tickets and everybody was like, that's really cool. They still talk about it.

We did a lot of stuff together, going to at least three cultural events per month, sometimes five. We got tickets for Steppenwolf Theatre, the Joffrey Ballet, the Black Ensemble, children's theatre productions. We went out all the time and people still really remember that.

I love the concept. Homelessness is very isolating and, unfortunately, the longer you're in it, the harder it is to get out of it, statistically. But Art for All forces you to get out of your environment and go into a larger community and be exposed to things.

And it can be interesting. You might be bringing somebody who doesn't have shower facilities and they know they smell bad and they're feeling uncomfortable. Or like there was this one guest and every time we'd go to a play, he'd snore so loudly. Now I've fallen asleep in plays too, but the snoring? I'd sit next to him. "Come on man, I got to keep you awake."

Venetian Night with the boat parade and fireworks is one of my favorite stories. I've done it for three years. One year we had a picnic and a lot of the alumni who I'm really close to were there. We were sitting on this blanket and we started singing songs from *The Jeffersons* and *The Flintstones* and all these TV taglines. Everybody was looking at us. And all these little kids started to sing along. It was so much fun.

It just frustrates me now because the Art for All coordinators don't even stay with the guests. They like take them to the play and they leave. What's the point in that? That's half the fun. And the whole point is to do a community outing and you're part of this community.

I think it's just because people are overworked and we don't have enough time. You work your butt off here. Everybody does. So I understand. And it's not encouraged like it was. This organization is changing a lot, for good and for bad. Organizations go through growing pains. You've got to respect what's happening. It's got to stay alive.

I don't know if you've been here long enough to have somebody disappear, when nobody knows where they are? There's like six people I can think of that are gone. I was really close to four of them. Nobody knows what happened to them. That was really hard.

And it's still hard. I'm not in the cafe as much this year. I kind of distance myself. And that makes me sad on the one hand because I have really strong relationships with a lot of the guests and alumni, only it's getting to be mostly alumni now. I haven't had the time or I haven't been in the cafe enough to really cultivate those relationships with the guests.

So even though I know that people still disappear, it's not in my face so much. I don't know how social workers do this. How can they keep working in this field and see so much of this happening? It's just…I don't know.

We added an Americorps*VISTA volunteer when half of the programs were being cut nationwide. That's a testament to the work we do. I think we have a very different experience than a lot of other Americorps*VISTAs do. Which is good, very good. We have real jobs. It's not a joke. It's a lot of responsibility for kids fresh out of college.

• • •

I came to Inspiration because of the dignity and respect in the mission. And while I thought that was so unique, I was also really frustrated. Why isn't this in the mission of every organization? It should be standard.

So, that's one thing. Anybody who's gonna start an organization, you need to put that in the mission. And if you're working with an organization that doesn't have that, you need to think about why they don't.

A lot of people think if you're homeless, there's something wrong with you. Our culture is so individual. You have to pull yourself up by your bootstraps. So it's easy for people to not think about dignity and respect. It seems obvious to them that the homeless don't respect themselves or otherwise they wouldn't be in the situation in the first place.

And then, the way things are structured sometimes, I feel like they're designed to keep people down. I don't get it. A lot of shelter systems, you can't come in after 6:00 p.m. and if you have a job, too bad. You have to choose between going to your job and getting a bed?

And what about the people who work two jobs but can't keep up with their rent? In Chicago, you'd have to work 120 hours a week at minimum wage to rent an average two-bedroom apartment.[8] Some family is out there, Dad's working two jobs, Mom's working one-and-a-half jobs, they're behind in their utilities, and who's raising their kids? Where are the family values in a society that forces people to do that?

We were raised to think that if you work hard enough you can make it. You can raise a family. That's the quintessential American dream. It's like an unspoken social contract. But it's not working anymore. People are working their tails off and they can't make it. That's not their fault. It's a societal crisis.

I just wish people would try to imagine themselves in other people's shoes more. If people did that, it would cut off so much crap. And it's so easy. Sometimes I can't get past how little people know of each other's stories, how little they are able to see outside of their own lives and their own development.

It's very easy for me to understand different perspectives. I grew up to be very literate. Reading gives you a natural empathy and ability to feel and imagine different ways of telling a story. I started to ask myself, "How would I be? What would I be like if I was in those shoes?" It's the most disturbing question I think I've ever asked myself.

I don't see anything in black and white anymore. Everything is gray. It can be kind of confusing sometimes. Things get kind of muddy. I have a tendency to over-story. It's very hard to find a balance between making excuses for somebody and trying to understand.

I love the stories but I don't take any excuses. A person is not the sum of their experiences but what they choose to do with what they've been dealt.

That was a really powerful thing for me to learn. Max is one of the biggest transformations I've ever seen in my life. He went from being the most poisonous person I knew to someone who writes poetry now. But back then, he was infectious, very infectious.

He and I spent a lot of time talking and I said to him, "You poison me when you're like this. I can't be around you because you're hurting me right now. I love you, but if you're going to be like this, you need to go. Do you understand how impactful you are to other people?"

I've had a lot of those conversations with people. I don't think most people recognize that their actions, indirectly or directly, have such a large effect on the environment they're in. Seeing Max's transformation was huge. He gave me a birthday card yesterday. I couldn't believe he remembered.

• • •

Sometimes I wonder who am I to be speaking about homelessness? Who am I to be speaking about racism? I'm a little white girl. But everything affects you, even if not directly.

It can be hard sometimes to work on behalf of other people. This isn't my story. This isn't my background or my experience. But, you know, it *is* my story. We share a collective history. Everybody's story is your story because we're all connected. I'm responsible for everybody else. You're responsible for me. All of our stories are connected.

I'm going to talk about this place for the rest of my life.

J.C. James

"I know just about everybody in this neighborhood," he says with a smile. "I care about people. I care about what happens to them." The air is crisp as we walk to the Weekend Center. A handful of people call out, "Hey, J.C." He stops, smiles, exchanges a few words, a hug, a spirited wave.

It came as no surprise to anyone that J.C. was voted Guest of the Month in January. He's known for helping out around the cafe and encouraging fellow guests and alumni. He talks with his hands and his eyes radiate kindness.

A few weeks later, he accepts a job as a sous-chef downtown. "I knew I was going to get it," he tells me. "I've been a cook all my life." I congratulate him. J.C. smiles, but his eyes seem to look past me. A cigarette trembles between his fingers. "This is just the beginning," he confides.

My story just might save somebody's life. You never know. Somebody might read this and say, "Hey, I don't have to go that way. I can change my life around. I can start right here."

I think it's very valuable to, quote unquote, let people know that the choices they make have consequences, whether they're good or bad. I'm not ashamed of my situation. A lot of it was realizing what part I played in being out here. This is my third time around.

I'm an intelligent person. I just have a serious problem dealing with drugs and alcohol, and life itself. I constantly relapse. And even though I work myself back into society as a productive person, when I relapse I only work on my strong points. This time around I told myself, "I'm going to work on my weak points. Maybe that's why I relapse."

Every time I start doing bad things—what you call cravings—I don't see them coming or I don't realize they're happening until it's too late. My wife tell me all the time, "I know when you fixing to go mess up." The people that really love you, they know.

You have to listen. You don't want to listen and it might take a while. I was always in so much denial. But now I see what she's saying. If I had just listened, maybe I would have did something about it. Maybe did something different. Might not have been my third time.

• • •

The first time I was homeless was in 1993. I was out here for a year or so. Got myself together. Got a job. Did well for a little while. But as they say in the world of Narcotics and Alcohol Anonymous, I found myself hanging around the wrong people, places and things.

When you get it together you want to go back to the old neighborhood. You want to say, "I look good now. I got away. I'm going to meetings. I'm working." And that's what throw me in the loop. A lot of people still know me up here. I might do well for a while, but if I keep coming: Wrong.

What happens is, you think, "Okay, I can come here. I can take a drink this time." You take a few beers, take a little shot, smoke a little weed. "Damn. I sure can handle this." The next time you come, "Oh, I did that quite well." But you just setting yourself up.

Doing those things, in that cycle, set me up to go back to crack. It was just a matter of time. And once you're back in those patterns, you get to the point where you don't care. You just want to get more of that stuff. You don't go to work. Don't call in.

I kept messing up. I didn't listen to my wife. She say, "Talk to me." But I didn't. You don't care. That's how you end up homeless.

Another reason I relapse is because I didn't work on relapse skills. I didn't ever really understand that there was such a thing. I've learned that nine times out of ten, you relapse from the same things. When I get myself together this time, I can't come back up here.

There's so much temptation. You find yourself doing things you wouldn't normally do. Sometimes you willing to do anything to get that drug, to get a place to stay, to keep warm for the night or several nights. I mean, it can be rough.

That's the sad part of it. Being out here will change you and in most cases, not for the better. Individuals that change for the better is few and far between, maybe three or four percent. It's real small. It's not a pretty life.

I got forty-five days clean. I take it one day at a time. In recovery, they always tell you to watch the places you go, the things you do, and the people you hang around. I'm finding out now that all those things can be positive. You just have to go out and find them, especially when they seem few and far between.

But they standing right next to you. All you have to do is just open your eyes. My eyes are open today. I get up in the morning. I pray. I ask God to get me through this day. I go to meetings. I pray some more. Stay around positive people. And stay away from people that's negative.

And even if you can't—that's one thing I realize—you *cannot* run from this stuff. You have to confront it. There's one word you have to learn: No. "No" is a key word. Even if you have to use it a thousand times in a day, say it. "No."

I walk down the street sometimes, "No. No. No. *No.*" So when somebody ask me, "Man, you want a drink? You want to smoke some crack?"

"No."

And when I see certain individuals coming, I go the long way around. There are things you just have to do and you have to do them on a regular basis. You got to do it every day. It's repetitious. You practice these things every day and as you do, you get better. That's why I think I'm not going to come back out here a fourth time.

I'm forty-nine years old. I know I don't have everything. But I can't do nothing about the past. I can do something about the future.

• • •

The homeless thing in this community is going to get worse. You know what I'm saying. Right now it's so easy to have all these agencies bunched together—medicine, social security, food stamps, shelters, places to eat. A person asked me today, standing on the corner shaking a cup, "Can you give me some change 'cause I'm hungry."

And I asked them, "Why?"

I know where they at. Uptown. Most businesses here, if you go and talk to the manager the right way, you can get a sandwich. That's what's so great about this community. They know there's a lot of homeless out here and they open their hearts and their churches.

When it get cold, they make sure you got long johns, hats, gloves. This coat I got on today, I didn't pay a dime for it. People in this community, they help the people out here. I think what they're getting tired of is the system that keep throwing more people out here.

It's the correctional system. We were at a forum for it the other day, talking about how the prison system disperses inmates the first year out of prison. They just drop them off in the community with no information, no knowledge, no help. Just drop them off.

And they coming into a situation where people haven't got their lives together yet, you know. So there's no hope. It's a chain. A revolving door. And there are so many young people out here today. They ain't twenty years old. Still wearing Pampers.

I also encounter a lot of people who I recognize from when I first came up in '93. They still out here because they get content. I mean, you can get content. You got three hots and a cot. Breakfast, lunch and dinner, and a place to sleep.

Every now and then, you can make a few dollars whether it's illegal or legal. Nine times out of ten, you don't have to hit nobody in the head to get it. Most people so generous they give it to you, just by asking. You can get food stamps or they give you SSI.

You stay in these facilities. Why get an apartment? Got a warming center from eight in the morning 'til seven at night. You can get to that point where you don't want to do anything for yourself. And sometimes it can be too late.

I tell anyone I see new on the streets, "Man, don't get content. Get your life together and go. 'Cause if you stay around here too long, you'll be part of the statistics. Part of this." I have grown content to a certain degree, knowing that if I mess up I can always go north and get three hots and a cot.

But something always seem to kick me and wake me up. I'm working on breaking that cycle in my life. There are groups where they talk about anger management, coping skills, living back in society, living in the community. I take advantage of those things. I need to work on some of those qualities. And it's free. Counseling, it's free.

I hope when somebody hears my story, if you have opportunities to get things free or when it's right in front of you, you take advantage of it. Don't let it slip by. I been here since 1993. It's 2005. Your prospects, as far as services, are not as good as they used to be.

When I first came out here, the services were a lot better. Maybe 2007, it gonna be worse 'cause it's not gonna be here. You see all the new condos going up. Everywhere you look at a vacant lot, condos or apartments going there. $230,000 to live there.

People have to wake up. I just hope some of these agencies that I talk about really start pushing that issue when they have people within their reach. They got to talk about how the community is changing. They got to let you know, "Hey man. Get it together. Change the way you think. Do it now because it might not be here tomorrow."

You see how downtown is? I mean, it used to be you could go downtown and panhandle and stuff. They don't allow that much anymore. There's a law against it. And you know the Pacific Gardens Mission, they moving that from downtown.[9]

It's an eyesore. People don't want it there. They moving us around. Spreading it out. This Uptown community gonna lose a lot of funding. A lot of things gonna disappear.

• • •

I volunteer here because this community—Inspiration Cafe, Rest Shelter, Uptown Ministry, Heartland Alliance—this community as a whole has given J.C. so much.[10] It's just a way of giving back, especially 'cause I'm volunteering with people I live with every day.

I know this man, this person, this lady. If they angry or they upset, they gonna come in with a mood. Some of the staff that work in this facility on Saturday, they not used to it. I am.

A guy came in Saturday. He was pretty upset. He had been outside for two days in the cold and he just wanted to vent. So come on, go ahead, vent. I'm not gonna get upset. I know how he's feeling. And that's what we need more people to understand.

We know what the person go through to come in here. We know how they feeling. We can relate to them. I won't get as pissed off as quickly as staff, you know. A guest might cuss a staff member out, and the first thing a staff member gonna do, he gonna go by the rules. He gonna bar that person for that day. And if it happen too many times, he gonna put him out the program. Sometime that might not be the answer.

When a person come in and I see he in a bad mood, I try to do a little one-on-one. Try to talk to him. Give him a little extra service. I been a waiter before so that kind of help out. You want to get a good tip, right? So you give that table a lot. Boom. "Sir, your coffee." Whatever.

It's the same way when you help someone in the community. You got to give them that special attention, especially if they been down and out. My mother always say, "Never kick a person when they down. You gonna kick a person, kick 'em when they up. But never kick 'em when they down because that's when they at their lowest point. And it hurts."

That's why I'm so active at the cafe. I don't mind helping out up there because they gave so much to me. That's what it boils down to. If they giving to us, we have to give back. That's why I'm here today sharing this with you. I hope when someone read this message, and when they get it together, they go off and say, "I'm gonna give back."

Have you heard of this movie called *Pay it Forward*? You need to see it 'cause this little kid got this great idea and it stuck with me. I love it. That's what I'm doing now. I'm paying it forward, hoping that somebody read this and pass it on, so two other people can pass it on, and two other people…. Maybe it might work. You never know.

· · ·

Two of my children married. All four have good jobs. I got seven grandchildren, all girls. I give that by the grace of God and their mom. I wasn't really there for my kids. They talk to me when they want to know about certain things they can't get from their mom. They know I know. So we communicate. But, now I'm just trying to be a good grandfather.

Family members tend to forgive but they don't forget. You know. I hope they let me back in. I hope my wife let me back in. We still legally married. Been together since high school. Childhood sweethearts.

And by the grace of God, if I get the opportunity to get back home and get back with my wife and have a good rapport with my kids, I can be a great grandfather. I love my granddaughters. And they love me.

I just want to work on myself, work on my recovery, and do positive things so I can be a great grandfather. I can show them a lot. Maybe be a part of their life so that they don't, quote unquote, go through what I went through. I can be there for them and kind of guide them in the right direction. Kids need that. They need some guidance.

My grandfather always say I was going to do something positive. I still don't know what that is yet. I did a lot of bad things. Sometimes I ask myself, "God, why you still got me here?" I'm still letting my wife down, my kids down, doing these things. But I feel that God got something for me to do. God has something for all of us to do, I think.

I'm just going to let him direct me. I'm going to try and do things for him. It's gonna be hard. I'm quite sure he's gonna send me through some tests and the devil definitely gonna come at me. 'Cause any time you start doing God's work, the devil gonna try to come at you.

So today when I have temptations, if I start thinking about drugs, I start praying. With God's help, he gonna give me the tools and the armament to deal with it as long as I keep focus on the right person. And that's God. He's my spiritual leader now.

You can't go into recovery trying to please somebody else. That's another mistake I was making, trying to do this for her or for them or for others. I didn't never really do it for myself. I did it because I want to keep my job for a little while longer, you know. And it didn't happen.

You got to do it for yourself. Put all these other people on the back burner except for God. God number one and you number two. That's how you got to look at it. Ain't no three, four, five and six. Because if you work for God and you work on yourself, you gonna start doing good things. Three, four, five, six, seven, eight just gonna fall in line.

So actually, I'm being selfish right now. And for that reason, I'm getting stronger. And everything else gonna fall in place. With my wife, you know, God's gonna make a way. If he feel me and my kids need to get together, he's gonna make a way. He want me to be a good grandfather, he's gonna make a way. He's gonna give me everything I need when it's time.

That's another thing, don't rush it. I always wanted things yesterday. I couldn't wait. I was too antsy. That's when you make mistakes. You start doing things to get things other than what God wants you to get. And God say, "He's not the author of that confusion." You know what I'm saying? You just got to take one day at a time. That's it. That's the message.

I'm not ashamed. Maybe in the beginning I was, because, you know, my family members and my mom, they always said I had great potential. But when you be out here so much, you can't get ashamed. 'Cause when you get ashamed, you hide. And when you hide, you can't get things done for yourself. I grew out of that. I accepted I'm an addict.

A lot of people come out here with pride. Pride can hold you down. Keep you bottled up. Okay, you made a mistake. It's just a mistake. If you make a bad choice, you can always fix it. Just do it. Don't keep walking around with pride and put on that, quote unquote, suit of armor. Sometime it be hard to take off.

I was told once—it was just maybe a year ago—that a butterfly, you know it start in a cocoon. It's ugly, isn't it? People walk by, "Look at that ugly thing on the tree." They don't know what's inside.

That's what being an addict is, that's what you become. A cocoon. A big old ugly thing. But inside, it's a what? A big beautiful butterfly that gonna bloom from all that.

When we come to abuse something so much, we put on that cocoon. It's a beautiful thing inside, but sometimes it get bottled up, closed up, thrown on the shelf and forgotten about.

So you want to bring that butterfly back out. It's such a beautiful thing when it fly out into the world. People say, "Look at the beautiful butterfly. Look at that."

Butterflies come in various colors, various types, various people. So, you know, I'm a beautiful person. We all are. I'm trying to shed that shell so I can bloom again. And there is hope. There is always hope.

Ask God to help you. That's the first thing you have to do. When that situation come, when it get really unbearable and you can't take it anymore, just get on your knees and pray. You keep praying. He'll know you sincere. He'll give you the strength. He'll give you the will. He'll give you fighting stuff to fight with. Just live in God. That's what it all boils down to, believing in him. He the only one who can do it for you.

Michael Mudd

In his characteristic jeans, black turtleneck and fleece jacket, Michael zooms to the cafe in his pale-yellow Mini Cooper. The sun is barely up over the horizon and he is off and running.

Michael volunteers, serving breakfast at the cafe several days a week. It's one of the highlights of his early retirement—taking orders, filling juice glasses, serving meals, and clearing plates. He knows everyone by name.

This is where I wanted to be. After working in the corporate world for thirty years, I wanted to do something grassroots, something intimate. Personal. I didn't want to trade a corporate office for a nonprofit office—not that there's anything wrong with that. I just didn't want that for a while. I wanted simplicity. Human contact.

I had a very senior position at Kraft, one of the top ten people there. And when you have a job like that you basically commit twenty-four hours a day, seven days a week. I worked very long hours and was often emotionally exhausted. And while I always thought about volunteering in what private time I had, I never found the will or the energy to do it.

Part of my responsibilities included Kraft's philanthropic program—about seventy-five million a year in food and financial support. So for about twenty years, I had the opportunity to work on the issue of hunger. I worked primarily with food banks but also tried to influence federal policy.

Knowing that fresh produce is the largest source of food surplus in the country, I started asking why the national food bank network wasn't getting much of it. And their response was they didn't have the right infrastructure. There weren't enough massive industrial coolers or fleets of refrigerated trucks, or food banks willing to become more sophisticated in their food handling techniques. Produce is a lot more challenging than just dealing with dry groceries.

And then there was also this really strong belief that at the end of the day, the clients didn't want it anyway. They wouldn't know what to do with it. And, there is some truth to the dietary patterns of low-income people. Fresh produce is enormously expensive on a per calorie basis. You get a lot more calories per dollar out of a hamburger than you do out of a pint of strawberries.

So that's what we got working on—funding the purchase of coolers and refrigerated trucks, funding the training for food banks and the educational programs that introduce people to different ways of preparing and serving fresh produce. Like this week, you know, we have squash and peppers and apples and peaches…. Here are some recipes you can use.

And, what was just so amazing about *all* of this is that the produce is *free*. Growers who had bumper crops and couldn't sell them were delighted to give it away. They'd rather do that than plow it under or pay for it to be landfilled. It's such a perfect win-win for everybody. And all it really took was about nine million dollars to get it started. So it was pennies.

By the time I left, we'd raised the amount of fresh produce flowing through the system by something like six hundred million servings a year. And that's not just for one year, that's on a sustained basis, year after year after year, because once the infrastructure is in place, the food can flow.

Six hundred million servings a year. Nationally. I feel great about that. How could you not? But I also felt like something was missing. I never had the opportunity to connect directly with the people whose health was being affected. The satisfaction I got was almost entirely intellectual. Not emotional. And that's what I longed for.

Goes back to my freshman year of high school. A theology teacher I had talked about giving—I didn't understand it at the time—but he talked about how it's easy for a rich man to give money. What's hard for a rich man to give is time because they're always so caught up in their own gig. To give of yourself is a much more genuine gift.

I don't mean to devalue what we were able to do. It was still a very good thing to do. And, it really made a significant difference in the quantity and the nutritional quality of the food reaching the hungry. It just didn't feel complete to me. Not that it kept me awake every night, but it was just this feeling of…of I know there's more

I need to do.

And to be totally honest, I was a little bit afraid. I lived in sort of a socio-economic bubble, not by any deliberate decision on my part but just by circumstance. I lived in an upscale neighborhood. Went to work at a wealthy corporation in a wealthy suburb. The people I came into contact with were all just like me. We were all so homogeneous.

I didn't know how to be with…with people who are different than me. I was worried about how I'd be perceived. Worried that I'd say the wrong thing, that I'd make a fool of myself or hurt somebody's feelings or just feel awkward and make them feel awkward. But all that changed when I decided to retire early.

That first morning here, I did feel awkward, like I didn't know what language to speak or how to relate. I didn't know how much it would matter—my education, my economic standing, my life experiences were so different from the people I was interacting with. I was respectful, but formal, too formal. Almost frozen.

But it didn't take long for me to relax. I think that's the key to this place. Just be yourself. I think the guests, more than anything else, just want to be treated in a natural way. They want to see that you're not patronizing them or bossing them around or uncomfortable with them in any way. There's nothing stronger than normalcy. You know, treat me like a human being.

And once you can do that, it becomes rewarding for both sides of the relationship. I feel totally at home talking with people now. It just feels natural. I don't mean that the difference has gone away, it's more how I feel about the difference. I don't feel awkward anymore.

They don't resent the fact that other people might be more fortunate in material circumstances. Just as long as you don't put it in their face. And it's, "God bless you. Thank you for everything you're doing to help me do better."

That's the most incredible thing about the cafe. We're not just giving you a meal—not just putting calories in your body—we're treating you with dignity and respect, and that's a very potent stimulant.

I think that's what keeps people coming back here. It's not just that I get some eggs and bacon. It's that with those eggs and bacon I get normalcy. I get treated like a real person. And I like it. I'm telling you, if these interactions make the guests feel half as good as they make me feel….

When I leave here in the morning, I feel like I'm glowing. The endorphins are rushing through my brain and I just feel happy. It's just about the best part of my day, being here. It's just the purity of these relationships, the simplicity, the honesty that I so enjoy.

I don't have any confusion about my role. I'm here to wait on tables. I'm not a counselor. I don't have any training in that field. So I don't for a moment pretend that somehow I'm supposed to accomplish something that a trained person can accomplish.

But I do think the value those of us who do the serving bring, is in how we do it—the quality of the conversation, our interactions, even the littlest thing like showing people the respect of knowing their name. Like this morning with Howard—I've done this every morning but this morning he noticed for the first time. I said, "Howard, what would you like?"

And he said, "Do you know my name, and I don't know your name? I feel terrible. I hate that when someone knows my name and I don't know theirs."

It was very sweet. I mean, Howard was a hard case for a long time. He was an angry man and for him to say that to me, it was just—that's what I hope these interactions can be, that in a very mild way, not in a serious way, but in a very mild way, they might be therapeutic.

When I think about how people are when they first come and how they are six months later, it's just remarkable. I see the anger melt away. They become so much more cordial and willing to smile, to talk, to treat us normally. So we get normalcy back. And that's great.

Like Joseph, I'm describing him completely. Recently he's been showing up every day, wearing a suit and tie, carrying this kick-ass briefcase. I mean, the guy is so relaxed now he doesn't need to push me around anymore or be angry in order to validate himself. He's getting the validation from within.

And when he first got here, he was almost frightened, unsure of how to even ask for a glass of orange juice. He was like, "Can I *really* ask?" And once he learned he could, he was like, "Hey! Get me some orange juice."

But now he's like, "Hey, how you doing?" He shakes my hand. "Could I have some orange juice?" And it's like, "You got it."

I fully realize that maybe .5 percent of the progress is attributable to our inter-action and the other 99.5 percent comes from the staff and the programs and the guests. But it's just so cool to watch. I mean to see a human being grow and find some happiness and self-respect. It just doesn't get any better than that.

It makes me feel more optimistic about the world. Like there's a chance, at least there's some opportunity for something good to happen, for some progress to be made somewhere, for differences to be bridged—even if it's only with a few people for a few minutes in a very small place, it still feels like there's hope.

And even though I'm an optimist by nature, I have to admit that the world, at least to my eyes, is becoming a much darker place. There's just so much hatred and violence and deceit and corruption. I don't care what part of society you look at, whether it's government, the media, even religion, it looks like the best of man is on the wane and the worst of man is on the rise.

It's hard not to get discouraged. It's hard not to ask the question, "Is there hope?" Is life worth living? I mean, if this is where we're headed as a species…. Most of us can't affect the world on any large scale. We just don't have the power or the influ-ence to do it. All we can do is touch the circle that surrounds us, the immediate circle, and that's good enough for me.

If I can't do anything about the big stuff, at least I can do something here. I know it's just a few people and it's a very small place, but to me, it's the world. It's my world. And it makes my life richer and happier to be here. It's very powerful to see people grow and change. I go home saying, "I got to see something really good today."

Zucchine A Scapece
(A classic of Naples, Italy)

Jonathon Goldsmith
Owner, Spacca Napoli

• • •

1	pound zucchini, smaller size
¼	cup extra-virgin olive oil
¼	teaspoon salt
¼	teaspoon ground black pepper
⅓	cup fresh mint leaves, torn
¼	cup white balsamic vinegar

• • •

Wash and dry the zucchini. Slice into rounds, no more than ¼ inch thick. Heat the olive oil in a small skillet over medium-high heat. When hot, fry the zucchini in small batches. Turn the zucchini over so both sides brown. With a slotted spoon, remove each batch as soon as they are browned. Allow to drain.

Place the fried zucchini in a bowl and dress with salt, pepper, fresh mint and vinegar. Gently mix. Allow to stand two hours before serving.

Serves 4

Jonathon Goldsmith and his wife and daughter have been a part of Inspiration Cafe for fifteen years. "It's easy to get attached to it," he explains. "It's a community. It works."

Over the years, Jonathon has prepared countless meals at the cafe, hosted guest and alumni retreats at his farm, and taken many under his wing. His pizzeria currently employs graduates from Cafe Too.

Chapter Five

⇥ LOVE ⇥

"There was a peace."
Tasha and Harry Madix

"I'm a mama!"
Tasha Madix

"It's a hell of a ride."
Harry Madix

"It's almost like a fairy tale."
Michael Korzun

⇥ Pears in Red Wine ⇤
Chef Jean Banchet

Tasha and Harry Madix

"Do you ever feel like you're not really alive?" Harry looks at me, rubbing his chin. "You know, like I can't believe all of this is happening?" An autumn breeze blows at our backs. A bulky set of keys clanks by his side. Two men standing on the corner ask us for some spare change.

Harry Madix is the cafe manager at Inspiration Cafe. His wife, Tasha, has just boarded the bus to pick up their son from school. Johann is five. Their daughter, Symphonie, is six.

I've spent the morning listening to their story. They weave it together effortlessly, each one building off the other, filling in the pieces, reminding. "We're on a date right now," Harry says with a smile.

Tasha

November 27 will be five years. We had nothing. Basically just the clothes on our backs. We worked together. Worked with the cafe. Stuck together through hard times. Sometimes very hard times. We just did what we needed to do to become a family and to stay a family. You know how people have their hometowns? The cafe was our home. Our base. The place where I actually found some clarity and started the process of becoming me again. I came February 28, 1996. I was twenty. Harry and I didn't get together until September. Our first date was at the Jazz Festival downtown in Grant Park. We met because of the cafe…and we stayed a family because of the cafe.

Harry

Our first date—it's been a while now—I know it was free. We didn't have any money. I'd been at the cafe about a year. Came in '95. Right around Thanksgiving. Was maybe fifty years old. Just something about the cafe that made me feel comfortable. It was like a foundation for starting over. There was a peace. A connection. Older alumni would come in for coffee and give us advice. And Lisa Nigro, she had a hell of a vision.[1] I just got tied in with some good people. Didn't know what the next day was going to bring. Wasn't any regular work, but they kept me busy. I told Lisa, "This is the first time I ever hugged a cop." Usually cops were hugging me with handcuffs.

Tasha

When Symphonie was born, I remember just worrying. Where's the diaper money going to come from? Are we going to have clothes for her? Where are we going to stay? The shelters were for women and children, but not for complete families. They were going to split us up, if we'd let them. We just had that stubborn attitude. Nothing is going to stop us. And the cafe really helped. It's such a stress reliever to know there's an organization that's behind you. One of the board members stepped in. Harry helped redo a basement. They offered that apartment to us.

Harry

Yeah, it was going against the grain of cafe policy. But we were out on a branch and it was breaking. We weren't married yet. We were so fortunate. No credit check. No security deposit. We fell behind there for a while but we paid it all back. Our landlord really stuck with us. Got a family himself, you know. Now we're looking for a house. Don't have a lot of money, but we can swing it, even if we have to eat beans and bean soup. Johann and Symphonie need a yard. They deserve it. Tasha deserves it, too. I'm getting close to retirement and I really want to get them set up in case something happens to me. At least they'd have a house. Won't have to worry about being homeless. I don't mind working for it.

Tasha

But this year I told him he definitely won't be working on our anniversary. Every single year it's been something at the cafe. We went on a date a few weeks ago. Only thing we could talk about was the kids. We tried to talk about everything other than the kids. You know. Same thing with the cafe. The regulars, the volunteers who come in every single week, they're like family. Johann calls Charlie "Shrimp Man." Charlie gave him his first shrimp and he fell in love with it.[2]

Harry

He sure did. See now, Tasha, everything's finally in place. We got all the jobs filled. Got kitchen staff, milieu managers, job specialists for Cafe Too. And now they're forcing me to take time off. Haven't taken vacation since I was a driver back in 2000. Went to this workshop three days last week and the place survived, you know. So I can start spending time with my family. Get some balance. Go on a date with my wife once a month. Be with my kids. The cafe is their life too. They thank the volunteers and cooks personally. They clean up after themselves. Take their dishes to the kitchen. We want to guide them toward gratitude. Everything didn't have to happen this way. It's not all about "me." It's about other people. Maybe something will work out good for them.

Tasha

That's right. Maybe one day one of them will be our future president.

Tasha Madix

"My story is a story of hope," she tells me. "How you can pull through despite the circumstances of your life." She brushes her bangs off her forehead. "No matter what has gone on in your past, you can be a new person. A good person. Eventually live a normal life."

You know the movie, *Lemony Snicket's A Series of Unfortunate Events*? It could be called *Tasha Madix: The Story of Unfortunate Events*. My life has had a lot of twists and turns. I had a biological family. I had foster families. I had an adopted family. I've had three last names and I've only been married once.

My mother didn't have a maternal instinct, you know. I was put into the DCFS system.[3] I went through six foster homes in two and a half years. I was six years old.

It's hard to take in a child that already has issues and memories of their biological family. A lot of foster homes only want little babies. There's a reason why you were taken away, and trying to make a child understand that the people they're with now is their family, is really difficult.

I was adopted. Found out later the only reason why I was adopted was so my older adopted sister could have somebody to play with. It wasn't out of love. My adopted parents just never knew whether or not they were going to have other children.

I acted out a lot. Basically lived with an inferiority complex that I wasn't worth anything. From the time I was eight 'til the time I was ten, I went to like five different psychiatrists. And every single time the psychiatrist would get to asking my adopted parents if they were showing me any affection, they would switch psychiatrists. That was a question they didn't want to answer.

So I had this complex like I wasn't loveable. Had to prove to everybody that I was. I was basically just…just a kid who didn't know where they fit in.

As a teenager, I didn't have that drive to do good in school. I'd purposely not do my work. My adopted father told me, "You're brain dead when it comes to math." I found out later that I'm great at math. But it didn't come to me until I was in tenth grade. I had a great teacher. I'll never forget her.

I had a couple of people who told me I'd do good. I took a child education class in high school. We had this mock preschool and I had to look after three kids. I loved it. And the teacher always told me, "One day, you'll make a great mother."

But growing up, my adopted mother always told me, "You don't have a maternal instinct in your bones. You're going to be just like your mother."

That stuck with me. I remember when I got pregnant with Symphonie, I had those thoughts in the back of my mind, "What if I am like my mother?"

• • •

I didn't come into contact with my biological family 'til I was nineteen. My adoption had gone totally bad. I ran away. I told the court, "I don't want to be there. Don't want to be in a home where I'm not loved, where I have to prove myself every single day."

The court sided with me. Asked me if I wanted to be in a foster home. I had no problem with that. I'd rather be in a foster home where I know the people taking care of me are just taking me in for the money. You know what I mean?

I remember one day my case manager came to my foster home and said, "Your mother has passed away." I thought it was my adopted mother.

"No, your biological mother." He showed me the obituary. Her funeral was in a couple of days. He asked me if I wanted to go.

I said, "Yeah."

At that point I'd already started trying to find my family. I had a list of names. I'd been going through phone books and starting to call people. Little did I know that my grandparents were living in the same house that my mom brought me to when I was born.

• • •

I met my family there at the funeral. It was so weird. I had this memory of my mother. I remember her long brown hair. I look almost exactly like her. I remember her running around. Her vitality. Her vivaciousness.

It was an open casket. I looked at her and it wasn't the same person. You know?

She died of AIDS. When she was in the casket, it was short curly hair and she looked so thin. That wasn't the person I remembered. That's not my mother in there.

I remember just standing there with my foster mother. My Aunt Donna—I didn't know her as my Aunt Donna at the time—was standing right next to us. She asked my foster mom how she knew my mom. And she said, "I'm here with her daughter, Tasha."

That like started a whole series—I was rushed from one family member to another family member. It was overwhelming. I learned that my Aunt June had been trying to find me for the last three years, you know, before my mother passed away. It was like I…I saw my roots.

And even now, there's still a half of me that's missing. I don't know my father's family. I know his name. I know what he did for a living. But I don't know that part of me. It's still out there. I'd like to be able to find him. I've tried. I know his name is Bruce Lester Peterson. I know he had a brother, Dwayne. Every single time I see a Peterson on something, I'm like, "Should I call? Could it be him?" Maybe one day I'll meet my father.

I know my mother's half of the family and that's meant a lot to me, to know the kind of people they are. And even though drug abuse and alcoholism run in the family, it's like no matter what, we know we always have each other to fall back on, even though we might not like each other's decisions.

There are still issues from when I first came back into the family. I didn't know how to act or react or anything. I had this understanding that they let me go. I found out my Aunt June had the opportunity to adopt me. But she didn't. That really hurt me.

I could have actually known my family. They say it wasn't good for me to see my mother do the drugs, the alcohol, go to jail. But it's like I could have been there. I could have known my brother and sister.

My brother and me, we found out that we're so similar. We get along great. He's mixed, like my kids, but darker complexion. We'll be walking along and his friends will be like, "Is that your girlfriend?"

"No, that's my sister."

• • •

After the funeral, I went back to my foster family. I was still in the DCFS system. One day, my brother called the house and my foster father got this attitude. "I don't want that n——— calling here again." That shocked me because I thought, "These are *my* people."

So I went to stay with a friend of mine. That summer, I got discharged from DCFS. My case manager pulled a few strings. I was nineteen. I went to live with my family.

It was really nice to stay in the house that was my first home. We all lived together, my grandmother and step-grandfather, my Aunt June and my Aunt Cecilia. It was weird. I remember the aunts sharing stories. I found out my Aunt June was like a second mother to me. So we had that kind of connection.

And my Uncle Jerry, he's only eleven years older than I am. At first his wife couldn't handle me calling her aunt. I remember him telling her, "That's my niece and if you have a problem with that, then maybe we shouldn't be married." They worked it out. She apologized to me and all that.

But it really was a learning experience to find out I had all these people that I could see parts of me in. I could see that I looked almost exactly like my Aunt Jodie. But I have some of my Aunt June's personality. Then I have my Aunt Cecilia's middle name. It was weird to see similarities having gone through my whole life seeing differences.

At the same time, it was like they wanted me to be a replacement for my mother. My mother was my grandmother's first-born. It was really hard on my grandmother. But the whole family wanting me to be my mother was really hard on me. I'm not my mother. I'm not some consolation prize you get with my mother passing.

It was like I was supposed to be…to be that rock. I couldn't handle it. I left.

147

At the time, I was working at the same grocery store with my Aunt June. I got off of work. Got my paycheck. Didn't tell anybody where I was going. I just left. Came to Chicago. Caught the bus from Rockford to O'Hare Airport. Didn't know anything about the city.

I blew all my money on hotels the first couple nights. Thought I was a party girl. I used to be bouncing off the walls. Had to be here. Had to be there, there and there. This place, the Weekend Center, was the party scene. I couldn't even walk past this building without going in.

But now, I'm okay. This building's just a building, nothing more than that. When I became a mom, I realized I wasn't a party girl. Basically never was. I just wanted to be one.

But even still…coming to Chicago was the best move I ever made. I was finally able to be a separate individual. I met Harry here. And even though I went back to see my family a couple of times, I never felt at home there. I knew something was drawing me back to Chicago.

Now I have the self-esteem to stick up to my family and say, "Chicago is my home. I'm the matriarch of my own family. I'm raising Symphonie and Johann to know they're loved."

• • •

I remember when I was finally able to look at my brother's father and tell him, "I forgive you." That was the biggest let-go of my life. I have this scar in the middle of my forehead. He knocked me off my chair when I was two years old. I hit my head on the edge of the coffee table. That's one of the reasons we got took by DCFS.

I knew I could forgive him because of one simple fact: He raised my brother to be a good man. And even though that doesn't totally erase everything that happened, it makes up for it. At least my brother was raised to not use alcohol and drugs.

And it's like I have that scar to remind me. I remember when I was finally able to pull my hair back and not hide it. I didn't feel ashamed. And *that* allowed me to have a good marriage, to have a good life, to actually feel good about myself. To look in the mirror and just see me, instead of seeing a person who was abused.

I just feel a lot lighter now. I can hold my head up high because I realize my mother did have a maternal instinct. I mean, maybe it was the best thing for me to be adopted. Just not into that family.

I made peace with my adopted father. It wasn't him so much as it was my adopted mother. She was the harsh one. They actually got divorced about a year after I left. We don't see each other, my adopted father and me, but I always feel comfortable calling him.

As for my adopted sister, we still have a relationship to this day. We haven't let all that animosity come between us. We talk. We email each other. It's nice. She had her kids after I had my kids. They're twenty months apart, same as mine. So now we are sisters by choice—not by blood, not by circumstance, but sisters by choice. And that makes it all the better.

But with my adopted mother, I…I just couldn't let go. I couldn't force myself to sit down with her. It's hard to have that kind of feeling for somebody. I'm just not ready to let it go. Her words affected my pregnancy. They were always in the back of my mind, "What if I am like my mother? What if I am?"

• • •

I want to foster Johann and Symphonie's dreams, to keep their dreams first and foremost in their minds. I want my kids to know they're loved for just being them. Sometimes they're a handful, but that's just being kids. They don't have to prove themselves. They don't have to get straight A's in order for me to love them. They don't have to go and solve the mysteries of the world or anything. They're just my kids. And that's enough.

In a couple of years, it's going to be on me to take care of the family. Harry's almost in retirement age. He's taken care of us since I got pregnant with Symphonie. That was seven years ago. We wanted one of us to stay home with the children. We figured as long as we keep scaling down and living with the necessities and not the "wants," we can make it on one income.

I think a lot of families put too much emphasis on the material stuff, having the high-priced condo, the high-priced car, the big vacations. I just don't believe that a person has to have a quarter-million dollars in order to be happy or to raise happy children.

I won't mind being the breadwinner once Harry retires. I hope I can do it without having to sacrifice spending time with them. I want to teach Johann and Symphonie that life isn't all about work, work, work. You can have fun in life.

It's still my dream to write. The other day, Symphonie was telling me about some dream she had about a monster that had ten everything, ten toes, ten eyes, ten…. I thought that'd be a great book. I like writing. It's something I can do from home and still be a mother and raise my kids. I don't have time to go back to school in order to provide for my children.

I'm also thinking about becoming a speaker to teenagers. I had alcohol hepatitis so I can't give blood or bone marrow. There are long-standing consequences to drinking and using drugs. Teenagers don't know that. They're not thinking about the rest of their lives.

• • •

A lot of things have happened in my life. But I'm comfortable with where I am right now. I'm a mama. I can sit down and talk with other mothers. I can sit down and talk with other wives. It's like I have something in common with all these people. I may not have a big fancy degree or big fancy things, but I feel calm. And I didn't used to be.

I've come down to a somewhat normal life. It may not be a Hollywood-style life or anything, but it's a normal life. It's a get-up-and-get-the-kids-ready-for-school kind of life. A regular everyday kind of life.

Normalcy. It's just that sense of normalcy. I didn't have that growing up.

Harry Madix

"I tell my story out of gratitude," Harry explains. "I've had a lot of help here, even when I think I didn't deserve it. I sit back and tell Tasha, 'Damn, Tasha. You know what? We got to remember where we came from.'"

I used to run away from home as a kid. Had to take care of the house and be responsible for my sister and brother. I'd just run away from it. Ended up in the juvenile system. They took me up to Angel Guardian at Devon and Ridge. It's called Misercordia now. I was in an orphanage, but I wasn't an orphan. I was just a runaway.

I stayed there from third grade to eighth grade. It was a Catholic orphanage. Predominantly white. I caught hell for a while. Made friends with an Italian boy and a German boy. We stuck together.

When I got there, I couldn't read. Couldn't write. Never stayed in school. At Angel Guardian I was blessed to have the same nun as a teacher. I really learned a few things from her. When I left, I had half a semester to go in eighth grade. I kept begging my mother to come get me. She finally did. Sent me to another Catholic school on the South Side. We'd already done the work they were doing.

Dropped out of high school two months before graduation. I was eighteen. Went into the Marine Corps. I was running away from the police. At that time, the judge was sending everybody into the service because Vietnam was happening. If you weren't like a mass murderer or something, they'd send you over there instead of taking care of you over here. You know, get their money's worth. That's the way I look at it now.

I went in July of '63. Was supposed to come out in July of '67, but I came out in December of '67 because I had to do five months bad time. I went to the Brig when I was in boot camp. They tacked on that time at the end of my tour.

Went to Okinawa first. We were supposed to be there thirteen months. After two months, they sent the whole division to Vietnam. Didn't even know there was a Vietnam. That's how much studying I was doing in school on current events. I didn't even know.

Got out in '67. Went to work at the post office. In '68, I went to Chicago Transit Authority [CTA]. Stayed at Howard Street for like eighteen years. Worked all the terminals. Helped bring in new trains. I worked with the old-timers. They knew the trains. They had a passion for them. Some kind of way, I got into that circle. They kept it kind of closed-off. Two or three other black guys actually got in. It was awesome.

But then I started drinking. I was drinking in the Marine Corps and I was drinking when I first got to CTA. Didn't even do pot in Vietnam. It was dope far as I was concerned. But I got back here, you know, and got kinda loose. Started drinking and drugging.

I got married in '68. It was rocky. I didn't know me. She didn't know her. We had two kids in the projects with the mother-in-law. The country was a mess. We had Vietnam. We had the Black Panthers. Dr. King got killed. I was right there, on the West Side, when they raided the Black Panthers. I seen all this and still didn't realize how serious it really was.

Ended up with a divorce. Then I married a lady from Evanston who really loved me. I didn't know what love was. She ended up getting murdered in a drug scene when she was in California visiting one of her girlfriends. I really went off the deep end. I was already an accident waiting to happen. Didn't have no balance.

I became homeless. Got fired from CTA. Could have got my job back if I'd went to treatment. But, of course, I was ashamed and I didn't have a problem. After a while, I wanted to go back. So I tried treatment. Didn't work. I was just doing it to get my job. I needed to break the cycle of using and I wasn't. Didn't have the desire.

So I traveled around, let's see '85 to…to '92. I was still homeless. Then I went into long term treatment in North Chicago Veteran's Administration [VA]. They worked with me a little bit. But it didn't work. I was still just one foot in recovery. So I went back out there until '95, until I got to the cafe.

I was homeless by choice. That's what I call it. There was a lot of help, but by me being a burnout, a workaholic and an alcoholic in denial all eighteen years of CTA,

I never knew who I was. Never learned how to set boundaries for myself. I was a people pleaser. With all those things pulling at me, I just checked out of society.

I wouldn't go to the VA to get rest. Didn't trust the government. Didn't trust myself. How could I trust anything? Even when I was at CTA, they had a lot of doctors but I wouldn't go down and talk. Pride. You know.

I know differently now. If I could do it over again with CTA, I'd say no. I was dealing with nothing but machinery and a time clock. At that time, that was okay. I didn't want to interact anyway. Give me my bottle. Give me my joint. You know. Then cocaine came along, and that was my love as I understand it now. Didn't know it then. It just had me.

Being at the cafe, I had the chance to get some balance. I stuck with Harry Rogers, the cafe manager, and Winston Craighead, my case manager. These guys were really into recovery. They'd send you where you needed to go. Detox, short-term treatment, long-term treatment if need be. And you'd go. Or you was out of the cafe. It was tough. Not like now.

Jonathon Goldsmith, Harry Rogers, Allison Miller [former board president], they really saved my bacon. I could always pick up sidework from Jonathon. Harry was my spiritual person—still is. He's my grand-sponsor and my kids' godfather. Allison always made a way. Kept us off the street. I was hanging with some fine folks.

We used to have a guest or an alum be the greeter at the door every morning. That helped me a lot, too. You'd check people in and say "Good morning." Might even change the other person's life. They might say "Good morning" back, and it might wake them up.

• • •

Then there was the idea of having another child and not being married yet. I just had a knock-around job. I never starved. My kids were never homeless. So when Symphonie was born, I remember Tasha saying, "How are we going to make it?"

I told her, "As long as we don't fall back, we can make it."

But I did. I relapsed. Wasn't making the meetings. Didn't have a sponsor. They say if there are any big changes in your life, you need to talk about it. I wasn't doing that. Tasha hit the ceiling. We worked it out. And, as long as I stayed halfway afloat, I had the support of the cafe. It's been good ever since.

When I was a driver for the cafe, I was meeting lots of people. Unbelievable. I mean, I was meeting people of the stature that I always wanted to meet when I was drinking. Wanted to be important. Now, it's just the idea of meeting people. I look at my contact list and say, "Man, look at this."

I've met Lester Holt personally. The Reverend Frank Lott from Lakeview Church called me like two weeks ago. He was on our Board. I just met this guy from Walter Payton High School. He's a science teacher, a black guy who did a donation with us over Christmastime. He said, "Harry, we got a lot of intelligent kids down here, but they're falling between the cracks because they have so much."

"Why don't you have them come up and volunteer at the cafe? Maybe that will help them get some perspective. I know Latin School does that. Parker School too."

We got a kid that comes from Park Ridge. Total introvert. Now he runs the grill like he's a regular chef. I talked to his father about letting him sit with guys at table ten so he could interact with people. Now he's all good. Drives out here by himself. Brings a buddy. I met his mother. Met his grandmother. The common denominator is the cafe. People helping people.

When I first became cafe manager, Las Vegas was taking bets that I wouldn't make it. I'm not surprised. They only had one alum, Richard Kelly, as a cafe manager. That was in the beginning when Lisa Nigro, the founder, was here.

And, after my first year, Lisa said, "Harry, it's getting to be spring. Are you going to stick this out?"

I told her, "I got to stick it out."

I'd never have gotten another job like this, with benefits, support and me knowing everybody already. I was very fortunate. They work with me. I used to blow up a lot. Anything could set me off—my peers, not having myself together, not getting enough rest. They really stuck with me on that.

Sitting behind a desk was a new thing for me. Completely new. When you're the new kid on the block, you got to roll up your sleeves. Got to get in there. Can't just dictate. Can't look down on nobody. Got to give and take, more give than take. I try to walk by example.

Change is hard. I came in through the old echelon where you went into treatment when you relapse. Now they send you through another organization. Which is okay. Got no control over that. Had to be my way before.

So it's learning to back off. Work with people instead of pushing it to be my way. Tunnel vision, you know. It's a lot better now. It's how I react to things. Most times, things are not that serious. Let's just get through this.

I'm with solid people. They have a vision. Goals. And, they go for them. To see the changes since Chris Persons [Executive Director] has been here, to be on the inside of all the planning, to be able to talk about it. I never imagined.

"Make a plan." That's all Chris tells me. "Make a plan and work it."

"Man, you wait 'til I get sixty years old to tell me that?"

But it's good. They guide me. I didn't know a damn thing about computers. Nothing. Was aware of them but shied away. I didn't want to go to college, and I could have. Didn't listen. Tasha, she took me through the computer. She knows more about getting around them units than I do. I'm learning. But normally, you supposed to come in with those skills.

It's a blessing to have a second chance, to be on the other side, to be with an organization that's actually going to wrap around you. Sometimes you might feel like you're just a number, but you still got to apply yourself. Got to want to do some things for yourself. That's what the cafe is about.

When I was drugging, I was depressed. Now, you can't pay me to sit on the couch for a whole day. There's no way. Don't care how cold it is outside, I cannot sit like that anymore. Used to do it constantly. Just sit. Go to a drop-in center, sit. Then get up and go to the next location. The spirit was broken. See, the spirit goes first. Then the mind. And then the body.

My mother always said I was going to be just like my father. Selfish. And all that time, my first marriage, my second marriage, that's what I was. Have to catch myself sometimes now. I can get to the cafe at five in the morning and stay 'til eight at night. If I don't set boundaries, my kids miss out. My wife miss out. My family miss out.

Never thought working with people could be so challenging. There's a different flavor for everybody, and everybody brings something different to the table. If it's not my field, I got to channel it to somebody else. How can I give somebody something I don't have?

But if I can help, I try. Not exactly giving money, but sometimes I do. A couple of dollars if somebody need a bus pass. Case management don't like that, but you know what, sometimes case managers are not around.

And I don't ask for it back. Don't have to. Somebody helped me. Somebody helped my kids when we didn't have a pot to piss in. For real. We didn't have milk for Symphonie. We didn't have food. We were living off of grits and a pound of beans.

But I still got up and I got tied into these guys. They kept me busy even in the wintertime. Worked with bricklayers. Never even made mud in my life. Mortar? You got to want to get up and keep moving. Have something going without taking any short cuts. Short cuts got me every time.

I tell you. This side of the fence is a lot better. You not rich in material things but you can sleep better at night. You feel better about yourself.

• • •

I call them the Symphonie and Johann Foundation. They're definitely known at the cafe. They get along with everybody. And they always want to help. That's the thing. I have to tell them to sit down sometimes. We teach them to speak to everyone, even the guests and alumni. You never know, you might make a person's day. Especially coming from a kid.

It's just one of the things I didn't learn. Say "Hi." In the city, when you ride the El or the bus, people are so serious. I used to be like that. Not enjoying the moment. Just going through life. Go to work, get off, run home…get up, go to work again. I mean, some people making so much money they don't even know how fortunate they are. They'll run you over on the street.

We're teaching Symphonie and Johann humility and gratitude. It's hard for

Johann. He'll cross his arms in a second. But you don't do that to your mother. Believe me. And as a black kid, he has to learn these things. Not to say that he'll be perfect, but he'll have the idea. I'm pretty strict at home but they still got leeway. We have discussions. We focus on listening. We talk about feelings. It's a way of life with them.

Symphonie's reading now. She's very interested in it. Johann's coming along. We read stories to them. They bring the books to us. They'll jump in our bed in a second. Sometimes we have to change beds at night. But it's okay. I didn't have a father at home. My mother was gone most of the time. I want Johann and Symphonie to enjoy life because I didn't. I didn't get a chance to grow up. I was a parent at five.

The only thing is they have to learn appreciation. We do the thrift store all the time. And Tasha picks out some damn good stuff. When she was pregnant with Symphonie, she got a new coat, a mother's coat. Cost me two hundred dollars. But she still has it.

I tell them, "You got pennies? Put them in the piggy bank." If you can learn to do it now, you gonna do it when you're older. Another thing I was told to do, but never did. Didn't listen.

But, it can still turn out for them. Might not turn out like we want it, but at least the seed is planted. Tasha *does* the job. She really does. Man, she went through more than I did. I remember creating my drama. She was more or less a victim, and then she began to create.

If you'd known her when she came in, you'd swear she wasn't the same woman. The lady was wild. Didn't wear socks in the wintertime. But Lisa Nigro and Harry Rogers, they took her under their wings. They seen something in her, but knew it'd take time. She's well-respected now. Stands her ground.

• • •

It is truly the journey. I understand that now. Not about getting to the goal, because after that goal is met, you got to set another one. Or else you just don't even exist.

I didn't anticipate being with the cafe this long. I can see where guests come in and disappear, not understanding the true mission of the cafe. Just coming in and eating. Not getting involved. Not understanding there's a lot of help here. Not benefiting from the food for thought. That's what I call it. Once you key into that, you start changing. Can't get that from a book. You got to experience it. Got to live it.

Without the kids, I wouldn't have focused on stability. Not even with just Tasha and me. It was a totally different ballgame once the kids came. They had to eat. They couldn't stay on no park bench. We couldn't be split up. And they tried. God, we was fortunate to stay together.

The way the world is right now, you can become homeless any time. Whether it's war, terrorists, fire, breakdown, burnout. Nothing is guaranteed. I understand that now. Don't care if you live on Lake Shore Drive—something can happen that can flip you. You might have money and still not be able to function.

It really was an eye-opener with the kids. You know. How do you explain it to them? And even if I might not want to do it for myself, they're there to put me in check until I realize that. "Hey, wake up. Damn fool."

It's a hell of a ride. It is. I'm gonna die at the cafe.

Michael Korzun

"I come to the cafe because that's where my friends are," he tells me. Homeless for three years, Michael works downtown now. On his days off, he greets everyone in the cafe with a hearty hello and then heads to table ten for some lively conversation.

This is the first time I have someone in my life that really matters to me. That's what it means to tell my story. She's the most wonderful woman in the world.

We were in this group at Thresholds. Thresholds is like a rehabilitation center for people with mental problems and learning disabilities. We went out once or twice. But then I got my room in the Wilson Building and she just didn't want to talk to me anymore. I didn't see her for about three years.

I was coming home from work and I dropped my bus pass. The 145 bus wouldn't wait for me, so I got on the 151 bus. Some cab driver had driven their cab into the Borders on Michigan Avenue, so the bus was very slow. And because of that she got on at Belmont.

I thought it was her, but I didn't want to say anything. All of a sudden, she went, "Michael. Michael. How are you doing?" It's been fine ever since.

I'm not a very religious person, but I believe that first time at Thresholds, God decided it wasn't the time. And it wasn't. He said, "You guys have to wait a little bit." He wanted it to work out. Wanted to make sure that when we finally did get together everything was cool.

Her name is Martha. I think she's the most beautiful woman in the world, even though she'd never believe me. She's incredibly brilliant. She reads a ton of books. I think she's got more books than the Library of Congress. And she reads them sometimes ten, fifteen, twenty times over.

Sometimes I feel like I'm not good enough. I haven't read the things that she reads. She keeps telling me I don't have to. She tries to convince me about how bright I am. It's working a little but sometimes I sort of slip.

She always says there are different types of intelligence. There's people intelligence. There's common sense. There's wisdom. And there's a good heart. That's the main thing. She says I have a good heart which is rare. And she likes that.

She loves poetry. She's got three poems published. I have this book of poetry and prose—most of them I never heard of—but I believe I found it in the lobby where I work for a reason. I memorized this song called "Afton Water." It took me forever.

I always want to do better. I write her poetry. It's not very good. But she says, "You wrote this. Nobody else wrote this for me."

We just have a good time. We'll rent a movie. Or the other day, we went to her workplace to pick up a package and then we walked through the campus and met a few of her co-workers. We sat on this little bench right by the lake and I read her some poetry.

See, she's rare. She really is. Sometimes I ask God, "What the heck did I do? What do you see in me that you brought her into my life?"

We're going to the Bristol Renaissance Fair and we've been invited to a wedding, her job coach at Thresholds. I have to go to a thrift store and get a buttoned-down white shirt. She's already bought my birthday present. Can you believe that? It's over two months away.

I keep two pictures of her in my Edna St. Vincent Millay book. I left it at her apartment so I went the whole week without being able to look at them. And, believe me, it hurt. Sometimes when I'm having a bad day all I have to do is open that book, look at her pictures, and I snap out of it.

A lot of times when I don't have a lot of money or I feel like throwing in the towel and quitting, I think about her and I realize that if I quit, I'll lose her. I can't allow that to happen. She's got me through some times that are just incredible. And I think I've done the same for her.

This is the first time I ever loved someone in my whole life. It's scary. My financial situation isn't that good. I was talking to a friend at the cafe who said, "Look at it this way. She's been going with you for almost fifteen months knowing that. She must really care a lot about you, enough that she doesn't care about stuff like that."

I try to accept it but sometimes it's hard. See my father was very old-fashioned.

He believed that a man should do whatever he can for a woman. It makes me feel bad that I can't do all these things for her. Money's not everything, but it does count.

When I'm going home from work, I see all these men getting out of these taxis with the girls under their arm. They're going to the Cadillac Theatre. I can't wait 'til I can do that for her. When I feel like I'm never going to have anything, she always says, "Right now you don't. But eventually you will. We'll work things out. Everything is going to be okay."

I know it takes a lot more than money. You can't hug a five dollar bill. You can't talk to it. It can buy you certain things, but there are things you can't do no matter how much money you have. There's a lot of people who have a lot more money than I do, and they have no one. They're not as lucky as I am to have Martha in my life.

She's everything to me. I don't know what I'd do if I ever lost her. I really don't. That's why I've got to control my emotions, especially when I get frustrated. The other day I stopped by her house. She was sick and I started pulling crazy stuff. And she goes, "I can't. I'm sick right now. I don't like to deal with that."

I asked her if she wanted me to leave and she said, "Yes." So I told her I'd stop and she said, "Okay."

See, you've never met her. One of these days, I'll bring her. I'll sign her up for breakfast. I brought her to the cafe like two or three times. We've had lunch, you know, the community lunch they have. Everybody loves her at the cafe.

It's almost like a fairy tale. You go your whole life and you never really had anybody in your life at all. And all of a sudden, because of a cab driver—whoever that cab driver is, I want to thank him, because if it wasn't for him, it would never have happened.

There's a place in my heart. I've never really let anybody in before. Martha's there. I just hope that it continues. I'm looking forward to tomorrow.

Pears in Red Wine

Jean Banchet

Retired Executive Chef, Le Francais

• • •

4	Bosc pears, not too ripe
1	vanilla stick
½	cup sugar
1	bottle dry red table wine

• • •

Peel, halve and core pears. Simmer in wine, sugar and vanilla until tender. With a slotted spoon remove the pears, place into a bowl and set aside. Reduce wine to almost half and pour over pears. Keep covered in refrigerator overnight. Serve cold with crème chantilly (sweetened whipped cream).

Serves 4

A veteran of many an Anniversary Dinner, Jean Banchet's first entrée into the cafe was preparing breakfast alongside Cynthia Brown, a volunteer for six years. To her surprise, he returned the following week with a box full of pots and pans to donate, one of which he'd selected just for her. The pan, she explains, did wonders in preventing her eggs from sticking.

Jean Banchet retired after forty-eight years in the kitchen. His restaurant, Le Francais, was named the "Most Influential Restaurant of the Decade" in the millennium issue of Bon Appetite.

Chapter Six

RESPONSIBILITY

"You can't give up on life."
Kimi Kahl

"I've always been work-minded."
Arnell Dupree Leggs

"I proved them all wrong."
Rodney Lewis

"I only ever thought of feeding the rich."
Jenny Urban

✧ Cuban Black Beans ✧
Chef Jenny Urban

Kimi Kahl

Kimi's long auburn hair is pulled back in a loose ponytail. Her baseball cap is on backwards. A set of headphones rests around her neck while her gray sweatshirt hides her White Hen uniform. "I have my own," she tells me. "I'm going home." A smile erupts across her face.

"In four years," she confides, "I told my fiancé I want a condo. It doesn't have to be downtown, just maybe out of Uptown. I'm tired of Uptown.

"He's like, 'Do you think that's possible?'

"'Yeah,' I tell him, 'it's possible. Anything is possible. The way you work. The way I work. Anything is possible.'"

Her eyes are bright. Her apartment is less than a month old. It's late December. She laughs somewhat nervously and then adds, "But right now, everything we have is going to the apartment. Everything."

I'm working downtown. One of the customers—she's a real nice customer—gave me the nickname Deli Girl. Now everybody thinks of me as the rich and famous Deli Girl! Working downtown, I run into classmates from grammar school, high school, and the short stint I did in college. It's amazing. I want my story to be told: who I am and why I'm at where I'm at.

I was born here in Chicago on the North Side. Three blocks from Wrigley Field. I'm the second oldest. I have an older sister. She lives in New York. Then it's me and my brother Eddie. He's my best friend. We're twenty months apart. If you were to look at us, you'd swear we were twins. He's just a giant version of me.

And then there's Justin. I named him. My mom had him at the age of forty. He's six now. I'm twenty-six. My parents separated when I was three. My sister lived with her dad and her stepmother all her life. She pretty much had a better life than me because she had a mom and dad for her. She didn't have our real mom. I had my real mom.

From Wrigleyville, we moved to my grandmother's two-flat. They converted the attic into an apartment and that's where we stayed. My grandma spoiled me and my brother to death. Whatever we wanted, we got it. See a Big Wheel on TV. "Grandma, I want that." You got it.

She passed away when I was seven. I carry a picture of her around with me. It's at home now, but that's because I got a home to leave it at, so I'm gonna leave it. But that was my lowest point so far, even being homeless. The lowest point in my life was losing my grandma.

She did everything for me. My mom wasn't there. My mom was lost in space, drugs, school, everything but having children. She had three children. She had my sister at fourteen and me at nineteen. It put a strain on her having my sister so young. It just tore her apart.

She didn't know how to be a mom. But my grandma did. So there you go. There's your mama. And we didn't have a problem with it because we saw our mom, so we knew who she was. We just couldn't rely on her for nothing. So me and my brother, whatever grandma wanted grandma got from us, because she was doing the same thing for us.

She smoked Marlboro Reds. I remember going to the corner store to go buy her cigarettes. This was when the corner store still accepted handwritten notes. It was one candy bar for me, one candy bar for my brother because we went to the store for grandma's cigarettes.

The day it happened, my mom and me and my brother, we were crushed. I was seven. I took it hardest of all. I was a very religious child. I told the priest, "My grandma's up in heaven. She's in heaven with Jesus right now."

I had a hard time when I went back to school. We had a week left of school, but I couldn't function. I was just crying all day. I was so used to going home and seeing my grandma. My teacher, Ms. Townsend, used to try and comfort me. She'd talk to me, "Everything's going to be okay, Kimi. Everything is going to be okay."

And I was like, "*Don't* call me Kimi."

"Why not? What's wrong?"

"That's what my grandma called me." Took me about fifteen years to get comfortable with Kimi again. I just couldn't. You call me Kimi and I wouldn't answer you. The way my grandma used to spell it, she put an -ie on the end. I took off the -e. Wanted it to be different.

So I made it through first grade. We were going to Walt Disney Magnet School up on the North Side. Great school. I love coming home from work because I take the bus and it goes right behind my grammar school. So I get to see it.

I completed high school and everything like that, but the biggest accomplishment was finishing grammar school. I was there for nine years. I thought it would never end. I was always getting picked on in school.

I really struggled in fourth grade. I had a learning disability but we didn't know it. I could read something but if you asked me what I read, I couldn't tell you for nothing. That's a problem. I'm still working with it today. Only now I can tell you what I read two hours later, two days later, a week later. But for a long time, I couldn't do that.

They put me in LD [Learning Disabled] classes to repeat my fourth-grade year. So now my mom had two fourth-graders in the house, me and my brother. They separated us as much as they could. But I wish my mom had let me keep on going. Holding me back just hindered me more. I felt like, "Damn, I'm stupid. I'm the oldest one in this class." I really did.

And when I expressed that to my mom, there was nothing she could do about it. I just lived with it. And it was hard too, being with my brother's people. It was always, "Aren't you Eddie Kahl's sister?" I was Eddie Kahl's sister for the longest time. That or Booger-nose. I didn't like being either one of them.

But when I went to high school, I realized people didn't know me as Booger-nose. They didn't know nothing about me. My advisor told me to be active, get involved. I took it seriously. I joined band. Basketball. Student Council. Anything that captured my interest and had no fees.

In the spring I went out for softball. Impressed the coach so much he put me on varsity and I never looked back. Played softball all four years. Basketball for four. Football for two. I was just a tomboy. Donell, my fiancé, can't stand it. I'm trying to outgrow it but it's happening slowly.

My junior year, my mom really flipped my world. She just decided she didn't like Chicago no more. My mom left. Packed herself up. Nobody heard from her for eleven months.

Then she comes back around, calls me on the phone. "Hi, my baby. How are you? Do you like where you're at?"

"Who is this?" I said. "I don't know you." I'm still in denial. She left me in late January and they placed me in a foster home. My case manager was always pressuring me to talk about my mom. And I was like, "I don't have a mother."

I never did have a mom. My mom was never really there for us anyway. So I looked at it like she left me. I don't have her. She don't exist. I wouldn't tell her nothing.

She said, "I'm going to make a trip up to Chicago to see you."

"I don't want to see you."

"Why not?"

"Because of what you did, Mom. That's so stupid. I don't even know why you left but you *left*."

My mom wanted me to meet her at McDonald's. It was down the street from school. I had the day off of work. So I went but I didn't recognize her. My mom was 300-some pounds when she left, and when I saw her that day, she was down to 105 pounds. And that was eleven months.

I knew something was wrong as soon as I laid eyes on her. You don't lose that much weight from dieting. Not in eleven months. I talked to her and everything, and we made a pact that I'd visit her for Christmas. She was living in Tennessee.

She really flipped my world upside down. I went through my senior year. I was nineteen. Got a job. My own apartment. Had a roommate. It felt so good. I graduated. My mom didn't show up. My brother was there. My stepfather was there with his family. My uncle and my foster mom. That was great. I wanted my mom there but she wasn't.

Five days after I graduated high school, I started college. Had a free pass for the summer at Northeastern. It was their Summer Transitional Program. I was like, "Cool. I can do this. I can hold down a job and go to school." My hours were flexible. I was working at K-Mart. It was great. I was functioning.

I called my mom, "I'm about to graduate from this program. Can you come to this one? You didn't make it to my high school graduation. Can you make it to this one? It's not as big, but it's just as important to me. It might not be to you. But it's important to me."

She showed up. It was great. I got to see my mom again.

Two weeks later I went to go into my counselor's office to get ready for fall semester. All my financial papers were in. I knew I wanted to be a social worker from the moment I was placed in foster care. I wanted to help young people like the people who helped me.

What I didn't know at the time was that my mom had went behind my back and applied me to the University of Tennessee. She had my social security number. So she got all my grants, all my scholarships to come down there. I had to drop out of college. I was crushed. I haven't really been back since. I was just so crushed.

My mom did the same thing with bank accounts. She'd come up here for little trips and put money in a bank account. She opened up a checking account with my name and overdrew the account by $375. Now I'm stuck where I can't open a checking account anywhere in the city.

After a while, I went to live with my stepdad. I couldn't deal with my roommate. And everything I had was going towards the apartment. So I went to live with him, but I couldn't manage. I swallowed my pride and called my mom up. Went to live with her for six months.

Then I turned around and came right back to Chicago. Now that I'm older I can tell it was drugs the whole time. That was her problem. She was using drugs. She started telling me I was worthless. And it's like, I'm better off in Chicago, in a homeless shelter or wherever I land.

I got a job as a waitress at a nursing home. Got the job through my old roommate's sister. I was working there, enjoying it. Living in a shelter. And then I moved in with this woman. She adopted me as her daughter.

The woman was great and everything like that, but then she started using drugs. And I was like, "Here I go again. I can't deal with this." I got out of there. Moved in with one of my co-workers from the nursing home. She was great. She had two little kids. I love kids.

We ended up getting evicted from that apartment. So I moved in with my boyfriend at the time. And he was, you know, he was demanding. Everything had to be his way. My friends and I, we called him "the no-good."

Then one day, I was coming home from work. I'd just bought me a whole new outfit—some nice jeans, some boots, a shag jacket. And this dude, he looked all right. He looked all right.

But I was like, "I can't be looking. I got a boyfriend at home." I look at him again. Then I transfer to the next train and he follows me. I'm looking at him and he's looking at me. And he says, "Nice jacket. My name's Donell."

The next day, he calls me at work. Asks to see me on my break. We sat outside and talked. It was October 27, 2001. He's like, "I would like to get to know you." So we made plans for our first date. I thought about that man for the rest of the weekend. Made my weekend. Went home to see my boyfriend and he's demanding dinner. I was like, "You can make it yourself."

Our first date was McDonald's. Our second date was on Halloween because we both had the day off. A few weeks later we moved into a hotel. Between the two incomes we were able to afford it. But then after a while it was too much of a financial strain.

Donell said, "I know this shelter you can go to." So he put me in the shelter. Walked me in the front door. We put our stuff into storage because it was one of the shelters where you had to lug everything with you. I hated it. I was there so long.

We couldn't get on our feet. He lost his job. Two months later we got news that the nursing home was closing. It was just like one bad thing after another.

And the shelter was very religious. I was real religious as a child, but it was like they crammed it down your throat. You had to go to three services a day and church on Sundays. You just can't cram that much religion into a person.

They didn't believe in men and women being together, even dating, if they weren't having intentions on getting married. At that time me and Donell, we didn't think anything about marriage. We joked and we said that's my fiancé, but it was just all in fun. They didn't like that.

I lost the job at the nursing home. I was a month shy of having two years when they let me go. They kept me 'til the very end. When I started I was making $6.50. By the time I left I was making $10.95. It was great but it ended just as quick.

I found a job a month-and-a-half later at a coffee shop. That was my first experience working downtown and I loved it, all these interesting people. But my co-workers started making it hard on me, and I lost that job. Found me another job. It didn't last. I was like, "Okay, here I go. Not going to last at anything."

By this time, August 2002, me and Donell was out of the shelters. We had bought a tent and started living by the river. There's like a strip of land by River City. We set up a tent there and camouflaged it. We lived there.

I landed a job at Au Bon Pain in September. It was great. I'd go into River City to use the facilities to clean myself up. Or I'd go into the shelter from time to time to take a shower. And we'd go to Catholic Charities for dinner.

We had a heater in the tent so we were nice and warm. With my income, we were able to buy propane for the stove and the heater. We also bought a car battery and an adaptor, like you'd take camping. Donell is ingenious. When the battery'd die down, I'd take it to work with me, charge it up and bring it back home. We lived there almost six months.

The day before my birthday, the tent collapsed. I was trying to get the snow off and I couldn't do it all by myself. It just collapsed on me. When I found Donell, he couldn't believe it. We got everything out that we knew we needed, stored it at his friend's house, and went back into the shelter system.

I hated it. Same shelter as before. They were so hard on me because I'd been gone for so long and I'm still with *him*. But there was something about him. The day of my birthday, he proposed to me. He's like, "We've been together for a while. We've been through thick and thin. Will you marry me?"

I was like, "Get out of here man! I don't know." But it was just like, "Yeah." So I've been engaged for a year now. Two years this January. We were ready to do it last week but we both got cold feet. But we said, "2005 is our year. We're going to make it official."

I went to another shelter out west. It was so much better. They were cooperating with me. I was going to work and everything. There was a clique of us. We're known as the "hooded bandits" because we all had hoodies on. I'm the only female surrounded by all guys again, just like my childhood.

And everybody in the clique knew I loved cooking. They was at Catholic Charities when Margaret Haywood from Inspiration came to speak about the Cafe Too program. All four of the guys came up to me, "Kimi, you got to check this out." So I did.

I went in for the orientation. Passed the math test and everything. But I had to ask my boss. That was the biggest thing I had to do. I was like, "I want to go to school and better myself. I can't afford college right now but there's this cooking school up north." I showed him the flyer.

He's like, "I don't have a problem. When you need to leave early, let me know the day before so I can schedule you accordingly." That's how our schedule was. It was never set in stone, not like White Hen is now.

So I came up here to Inspiration Cafe. My boss was very pleased to have me going to school. But my supervisor was jealous. After a while, they started to notice little changes in me and that school was taking over my coming to work. They didn't like it. They let me go. Told me I had to get my stuff.

I had stored some of my stuff in the lockers because I had no room at the shelter. We were able to leave our stuff there, but I was still in stage one. I only had two bins. Stage three, you get three bins. But I wasn't there yet.

So I called up the cafe. Told them I was going to be late. I called back to the shelter and said I'm on my way home with my stuff. I cried so much. Here I am trying to better myself and you fire me. That ain't right.

I called Donell at school. Told him what happened. He said, "Go home. You'll find better. Go to school tomorrow. Don't worry about it." Amalea and Sharon, the two chef trainers said, "God's going to bless you with something bigger and better."

Two weeks later, Harry Madix comes up to me. "Young lady, what's your name?"

I was like, "I'm Kimi."

"You're just the lady I'm looking for. Are you still looking for work?"

"Yeah."

"I got a position for you." He hired me that day. July 18. So within two weeks of being fired, I got a new job working for the cafe: kitchen assistant. And then I became a kitchen coordinator.

I was right in the middle of Cafe Too. I started dating food and cleaning up the kitchen after the volunteers, like Charlie on Friday mornings. That's when I met you. You met me when I first started working up at the cafe two summers ago.

Amalea and Sharon were right. I found better. I found Soldier Field. From Soldier Field I went to M&M Mars, which didn't last because I couldn't get up at four in the morning. Transportation was a problem. I was laid off for a little bit. And now I'm at White Hen.

Been at White Hen since August. Moved up from assistant manager to deli manager. It's the best job I've had since the nursing home. I'm downtown, meeting all kinds of interesting people. There was one guy who walked in and he's like, "You look familiar. I've seen you somewhere." We both graduated from Cafe Too. It all ties in.

Now I have my own apartment with Donell. Nice little studio to call my own. It's great. It's small but big enough. Our kitchen is huge. We realized that yesterday when we were rearranging our blankets. We try to switch them around so we can sleep better trying to find the right position. We just need some furniture.

But I love having my own. I wouldn't trade it for nothing. And I wouldn't trade Donell for nothing. At times he gets me upset about things he does, but he's my best friend. I'm proud to say he's gonna be my husband.

And now that I got my apartment, I'm slowly drifting myself from the cafe. That's not everything I'm about. At one time it was everything I did: Cafe Too, kitchen coordinator, guest/alumni council.

I'll always remember the cafe 'cause that's where I met so many great people. That's what makes Inspiration *inspiration*: the staff, the volunteers, the clients working together, trying to rely on each other because staff can't always do everything you need. You do need your peers. And in my case, my older peers. I'm the baby of the cafe.

My experience has been a rough one. But it's made me stronger. Everything has made me stronger. My mom, you know, everybody else would have disowned her. Donell don't understand why I talk to her, but I do. That's the woman who gave birth to me.

I spoke to her on Christmas. It was a hurry-up-and-get-off-the-phone conversation. But I did it because I'm the bigger person in the family. And I don't give up on life. That's one thing I've learned. You can't give up on life.

• • •

At Alfred Smith's memorial service, Kimi shared with all those who gathered, including Alfred's two sisters and niece, that Alfred had taught her mother in grammar school. He also taught all of Kimi's uncles and knew her grandmother quite well.

Arnell Dupree Leggs

Walk into the kitchen at The Living Room Cafe and the first person you'll meet is Arnell. In his standard baseball cap, button-down shirt and baggy jeans, he welcomes you in. He asks you to don your own white apron and hairnet and makes you feel right at home, even if you've never washed greens, chopped onions or fried fish before.

I've always been work-minded. My mom had us cooking at the age of eight. My brother and me. We're twins. Arnell and Darnell. We always worked around the house—cooking, cleaning, shoveling snow, raking leaves. Everything. But cooking, I fell in love with it.

We grew up in Chatham. A middle-class neighborhood. My mom worked for the Chicago police. My dad for a trucking company. During my high school years I worked at the alderman's office. He was our neighbor. Grew up with his kids. He kept me and my brother with a job—filing papers, folding flyers, cleaning up streets. Got paid minimum wage, $4.25 back then.

Did that all the way through high school. Me and my brother gangbanged. Worked during the week and went to meetings on Friday nights or Sunday mornings. We was wild. Seen a lot of my friends get killed. Wrong decisions. Stupid life decisions they made.

I graduated from high school. Worked for Chicago Board of Elections. Did that almost three years. Left there and went south. Stayed in Atlanta and later Alabama for a bit. I was twenty-two. Came back here and got on my feet again for about a year and a half.

Worked for Dominick's Finer Foods, bagging groceries, pushing carts. Had a commute that was two hours. Two trains and a bus. Worked out there five days a week, seven hours a day. And two hours on the way back home. Did that for almost two years.

Left there and became homeless for like six months. Couldn't believe it. Never thought about being homeless until it smacked me right in the face. Pow. Homeless.

People was like, "Get you a job." But I couldn't. I couldn't get a job for nothing.

One night I got to crying. I could always get out of a predicament. But not this time. And, it was hard. Being homeless is no joke. We were out on the street. It was cold. My brother caught frostbite. That was the worst time of my life.

I love my brother to death. But damn, it was my fault. I left my job. I made that bad decision. Got upset and quit, not knowing it was going to hurt anybody but me. We shared an apartment and my brother was dependent on me to keep my job so I could help pay the rent.

I just had a bad attitude. I work hard, but if somebody make me real mad, I leave. Hell with that, you know. Most people find a job and work it. Me, I get upset and leave. But I'm learning to control my attitude. Take the feedback, advice, whatever, and just keep doing my job. Leaving ain't the right way to go.

Me and my brother, we went up north. Found Inspiration Cafe. Found out they had free cooking classes, so we didn't mind that. It was twelve weeks. Met a lot of good people. Slept in the back of my friend's garage and graduated from Cafe Too. Both of us.

Left there. Worked at Nieman Marcus as a dishwasher/prep cook. Did that for about a year and a half. Left there. Worked at Popeye's Chicken. Oh my God. That's the roughest job in the world. People be so rude to you. I wasn't making enough money so I needed a second job.

I went back to Inspiration Cafe. My job counselor, Ms. Jeannette Blackwell, she's a very sweet lady. She said, "Oh, we got a job right where you at—at The Living Room Cafe."

I was like, "The Living Room Cafe? On 64th? I can do that." I used to come out here delivering stuff with Harry. And that's where I've been now for the last few months. I'm the kitchen coordinator.

I check all the food, help prepare meals, help the volunteers out, if they come in with they own food or cook what we have. Take care of the kitchen and the volunteers. That's what the job consists of. Make sure everything gets done. Make sure the cafe is okay.

I'm staying with my sister right now, so you might as well say I'm homeless 'cause if my family ever get to tripping, I'd be homeless. That's the thing. She got her own little issues. So I'm like one foot in and one foot out. Makes me think about uplifting myself even faster.

I done a lot of wrong things. But I also done a lot of good things too. Working here is one of the good things. Cooking for people who are homeless. And for the past four years, I've volunteered with my church to pass out food on Christmas.

My mom's in Tennessee. My brother's in Orlando, Florida. I got a gang of nieces and nephews and cousins, though, who love to see me. I take them out. Do whatever they want to do. I'm game. 'Cause I'm thirty. I'm still like a big kid. I think I need to start growing up a little bit. Stop being so cool.

I'm single. Never been married. No kids. Looking for Ms. Right. Feel like I let her pass me up already. But hopefully she'll come along, you know. I'm still kicking with my guys. They like my other family. Sometimes I get depressed and I don't have nobody around to talk to. But I can always hang with my guys. I appreciate that.

I learned a lot from being homeless. I learned that if you need something, you got to let your pride go. If you know you need help, then it's good to ask for help. If you think about it, these places are out here to help people. I had to let my pride go.

Being homeless also taught me never to judge a person. That's the real thing. I got out. Made myself a better person. And I'm learning to still help out people who are homeless. I don't mind. It takes a big person to realize their mistakes and fix them, instead of keep making the same mistakes.

I tell anybody, "Don't give up. Your life can change. It can't get any worse. It can only change for the better. And if it do get worse, then there's something in your life that you're not doing. But don't give up. Thank God. Because He don't put too much on your plate that you can't handle."

A lot of volunteers come in here and I want to thank them. Any volunteer that come in here and help Arnell prepare a meal, push that meal out, or any volunteer who brought meals in, thank you from the bottom of my heart. You're helping people in this organization. And I thank each and every one of you.

Rodney Lewis

"Come on, I'll buy you breakfast!" he says as he holds the cafe door open. I see the women chuckle at his offer. There's a lightness in their step that wasn't there a minute ago.

Rodney came back to the cafe in March. When we first spoke, he'd been a guest for exactly one month. He was working Earn Fare, washing dishes at a local social service agency, and trying to catch up on his sleep. He gave up his spot to sleep at the Weekend Center so we could talk.

I just come out of prison. Did eighteen years. I went into prison when I was twelve years old and I got out when I was thirty-one. Been locked up a long time. Did five years in juvy and then when I turned seventeen, I went into an adult prison. Been in twenty-eight prisons in my time. I got fortunate. Got my GED and sanitation license out of it.

I been out of prison seven years now. My mother—I call my auntie that raise me my mother—and my uncle, they died while I was in prison. And my family, they stay in parts of D.C. I could have went back to D.C., which I did, but I didn't like it. So I came back to Chicago. I like Chicago. Been here all my life.

Life was crazy when I got out. I just come out of being deprived. Being locked up every night. Being expected to go to my bunk every night. Being counted. That's all I knew for eighteen years. Be here. Be there. Be counted. Then all of a sudden, I didn't have to do that no more. It's a big change. I was just wild, that's all. That's what brought me here. It's better being on the streets than being locked up.

I've stayed in different shelters. Stayed at Rest. Breakthrough. Salvation Army. And, the times when you don't got nowhere to go, you sleep where you can. In a park. On the train. Being here. Being there. That's what I been doing for the last seven years, going back and forth. I been working here and there. Now I'm working at Salvation Army. I wash dishes for them.

I had some trouble. Ended up being HIV. I be messing with this girl and I didn't know she had it. She didn't tell me. I'd get tested and I kept testing negative. Then all of sudden, I test positive. When I found out, I had something like 57 T cells and my bi-low was 37,000. That's like, very sick.[1]

So then I started getting into this place called Chicago Health Outreach. It's across the street. They take people if they HIV or they homeless or they can't afford nothing or they ain't got no medical cards. If you sick or something, you can go over there and get medicine. That's where I get my HIV medication.

But when I found out, I started getting high more. I say, "You fixing to die anyway, so it doesn't matter." That's what I thought at that time. So I kept getting high and my bi-low kept going up and my T cells kept going down. My case worker said, "Taking this medicine ain't doing no good if you getting high. It ain't gonna work."

I figured I ain't got nothing to lose no way. So what the hell. I gave myself ninety days to stop being high. I wasn't going to do nothing for ninety days and see if this medicine work. And if the medicine work, then I'll stop getting high. This was like fifteen months ago.

When it was time for me to take my labs again, I hadn't got high in ninety days. My bi-low went to undetectable and my T cells went from 57 to 112. Ninety days after that it was still undetectable and my T cells went to 300 and some. Another ninety days, my T cells were up to like 625 and I'm still undetectable. Been undetectable for almost like eighteen months now. So it's working a little bit. It's getting better and better.

But then it went down a couple of times as me being homeless. I have nowhere to sleep. It's not really cool to be out here like that. I take medicine twice a day. I take Combivir in the morning and Sustiva at night. I just go to sleep where I can or I get in the shelter if I'm not cut or nothing. If you cut, then you got to ride the train all night. It's kind of hard. I'm tired.

My hope is to be up off these streets so I can rest my body like I want to rest it, not like going in and out of these shelters. You go in at night and you got to be up at six o'clock in the morning and go. It's like sleepwalking.

I really don't want to go to these shelters no more, but right now, I really have no choice. I got into the cafe. I got Nell McNamara for a counselor. They need more people like her. She been helping me real good, helping me find a place to stay. She got a lot of leads. And she won't let me do no goofy stuff. She ain't been doing nothing to let me slide.

And I been doing everything I supposed to be doing. I'm not really trying to find out what a bad angle is. I'm not looking for the easy way out. I just keep it like that. I keep doing what I'm supposed to do and she keep doing what she supposed to do.

That's what I learned. People just don't jump 'cause you think they should jump. That's the kind of stuff I used to get mad about. They just tripping my way. Now I know life is like that so I don't get angry too much.

Things don't always move my way every time I go for something. 'Cause of my background, something always snag me. It's kind of hard that the mistake I made when I was twelve, I never knew it'd follow me the rest of my life.

I'm just trying to come back. Been out of prison for seven years. Haven't been back for nothing. And I'm not going to get myself locked up for nothing. Already been through that. I did some bad things when I was a kid and I did eighteen years. I had forty years.

I'm not on parole or nothing. I'm not on probation. I don't mess with the police. If they stop me, they run my name. They see what I was locked up for and they get kind of offended by it. But other than that, they stay out of the way. I'm just free.

• • •

Three weeks pass and one morning at breakfast, Rodney tells me he wants to tell me more. He wants to tell me what happened to him when he was a child. My tape recorder is in my bag and we find an empty office to sit in. I tell Rodney to start wherever he wants to start.

All right, I'll start when I was twelve. I had, ah, got in some trouble.

I killed somebody when I was twelve.

I started hanging with the wrong crowd when I was eleven. I used to hang around this other guy. He was making something like $30,000 a day. He was selling T's and Blues. They shoot them in they arms. So, I used to hang around with him. I see he had a gun on the side.

One day, he was going to do something. He say, "Hey, Rodney. Keep this stuff and I'll be back later on." That's when he gave me the gun. That kind of frightened me. I had a gun, you know. I had power. See what I'm saying. Soon as somebody tell you something crazy, then I pull it out. "Motherf—, I blank-blank-blank you." Something like that. That's how it went.

So from then, I just walking around thinking I'm a bad ass with a gun on my side. You know what I'm saying. Eleven years old. I used to make runs for them. Made me a few dollars. I walk around with a gun and maybe four or five hundred dollars in my pocket. At the age of eleven, that was power. I seen he wasn't getting caught. I mean, man, that's what I wanted to do.

I brought him home one day. My mother, she didn't like him. Didn't none of my family like the idea of me hanging around this guy. His name was Rodney, too. It was like five of us. Five Rodneys, we used to hang together. I'm the only one living.

My mother, my uncle, they tried. They tried to stop me. But I didn't listen. I didn't want to listen to that crap. Not at that time, you know.

We were at two young ladies' house, two sisters who share the same place. I seen the guy the day before. I was trying to go over there to talk to him. He came up to me and he…he pulled a gun out, put it in my face, and clicked it.

It just so happened, the gun didn't go off until he put it back down. And when it went back down, it shot a whole pile of concrete about fifteen feet in the air. So that kind of scared me. I ran across the street. My partner had a gun. I ran back inside and emptied it on the guy.

• • •

He's quiet for a moment. His eyes are downcast. I ask him, "So, that's what happened when you were twelve?"

183

Yeah.

And, in the process of that, the police was trying to get me. I ended up shooting two officers because they was trying to shoot me. They shot at me first, and I just picked the gun back up and shot one of them in the back and one in the stomach. I got forty years for that.

And, it ain't been all that good coming out, either. I mean, I just don't want to go to jail, you know, so I don't try to put myself in that predicament. Don't do nothing crazy. Don't get me wrong, a lot of people—a guy come up to me the other day with something stupid. He had a plan or something. Whatever it was, I wasn't interested.

I calmed down a whole lot. For the people that know me, they'll tell you I calmed. I'm still angry, but I'm just not acting the way like I used to. I know that ain't the way to go. I used to fight. I fight to win.

When I was in the penitentiary, I had got the guys so scared of me that this guy, he took a forty-five-pound plate and bust me upside my head. I had like forty stitches and twenty staples. He almost killed me with that.

So I stopped. I stopped trying to intimidate, you know. People knew I could fight. They knew I was kind of scaring these guys and all that crap. I figure, if I had been on the street, he probably shot and killed me. You know. So what I do now is I just don't…don't react to it.

I got stabbed when I got out the penitentiary. I been out thirty days. They tried to kill me. They tried to get even. The guy I killed, his brother in a gang. So they snuck up behind me.

Other than that, I been cool. Just been lucky the last seven years. I mean, it ain't terrific but it been all right. I ain't been stabbed, shot, none of that kind of stuff, since. The last incident was six years ago. So I ain't been in no trouble. I ain't hung around nobody that do that stuff.

That one time when I was twelve, you know, it just took everything I had. My juvenilehood. My adulthood. And everything else. That background's hard to get any kind of job. I got a murder and two attempted murders against the policemen. I got hard violence.

They do background checks from the time you was locked up. I stabbed a couple of guys when I was in prison. So my background got a lot of violence in it. And, if you look at what's going on in Atlanta—where the judge got killed—you got a lot people doing crazy stuff.[2] I guess an employer don't know how I'll react if something happen. If I'm gonna go get a gun and shoot everybody in the place up.

I just don't know sometimes, you know. Sometimes I sit down and think my life is over. I feel my life should end. I ain't gonna hurt myself. I don't do that. And I don't want to hurt nobody else either. My eyes open now. You ain't got to solve nothing by fighting all the time. I don't want none of that kind of crazy stuff. It's just, I'm…I'm tired of society sometimes.

When I talk with people, I try not to talk with somebody who feel sorry for me. I don't like that. A lot of people, you know, when they hear a guy's been locked up since he was twelve, they think he'll be back in jail. Give him thirty days. They say once a person get out, if they spent a long time locked up, they gonna be back.

I prove all them wrong. I prove them wrong almost eight years now. But when I start talking, a lot of people already judge. You know what I'm saying. They smile in your face and then when they get behind you, they start talking. They getting down, you know. So I have to go with the flow.

Just keep on. Every time I wake up and I'm not in the penitentiary, that's motivation. That keep you going, even though things ain't going good. I ain't got a job. I ain't got a place to stay. But it don't make me want to do nothing crazy. You know what I'm saying.

Stealing and robbing weren't my thing, no way. My thing was I like to play with guns. But it wasn't robbing or sticking up nobody. It was just, I guess at that time I just…I just didn't care. I thought everybody was out to hurt me, so I want to hurt them first. You know.

I know I don't want to die. And I know if I'd kept doing what I was doing, I know that time would be there. Somebody would have got me. Then again, somebody still might but it won't be because of me out there acting crazy.

• • •

185

Twelve-year-old boys need to stay in twelve-year-old boys' places. They need to not be trying to hang around nobody that's destructive like myself at that time. Eleven and twelve-year-old boys, you can talk them into doing *anything* and they'll *do* it. Lot of them try to act like they hard-headed, but they not. They fold over like a pancake.

They still twelve-year-old boys. They get in front of the judge, they think the judge going to show them sympathy. They start crying and all that old crap. The judge gonna give you more time. So, listen to your mom. Listen to her.

If not, she'll be looking back at you when the judge and the prosecutor keep telling her how dangerous you is to society. "You had no business carrying guns. You had no business being around drug dealers. You had no business, this and that. You a menace to society."

If my story help somebody, you know, that's cool. Give it to a twelve-year-old. They never listen to they parents. And, if they always getting in trouble, then they'll know about life in a penitentiary. It's not easy to go through eighteen years of prison. It's not easy at all.

Just remember, you choose. You gonna bring it on yourself. You choose to do good, you gonna do good. You choose to do something bad, if you lucky you can do eighteen years but if not you end up dead. Whatever choice you make, make sure it's the choice you want.

Jenny Urban
"Chef Jenny"

The cafe is packed this evening. Family members and friends gather around the graduates, listening to their stories from the past three months. Flowers and balloons garnish the tables. Cameras flash.

Tonight's meal is a rite of passage. The graduating Cafe Too class designed the menu and the incoming class prepared it. Chef Jenny assures me the food will be amazing: corn chowder, mesclun salad, barbeque short ribs, garlic mashed potatoes. Looking around, she adds, "Everyone is so dressed up. They look so professional, so confident."

After the dinner, testimonials and parting speeches ease our full bellies. The last graduate to speak tells us, "I now know what inspiration means." Applause fills the room. I find Chef Jenny and see an unmistakable mist pass over her pale-blue eyes.

If you'd asked me a few years ago what I planned on doing with my culinary degree, my answer would have been simple: "I'm going to work in a fine dining restaurant until I can afford to open my own."

That's all you think about in culinary school. It kind of engulfs your mind, feeding the rich, making it nicer, more expensive. I remember selling a thirty-five dollar plate of food and thinking, "Wow. I'm really important now. Somebody just bought this and it's like five dollars worth of food." Those thoughts almost haunted me. Bigger. Better. More.

I got an opportunity to come to Chicago after graduation. Everything was going my way. Felt like a hotshot culinary graduate moving to the mecca of fine dining.

But everything changed once I got here. My field was grossly saturated and I was just one of the many that had a degree and experience and a drive for fine dining. I was sending out like twenty resumes a day with no reply. Moving back to Kentucky was not an option so I was forced to accept a couple of jobs that were not culinary related.

A few months later, I got a call from Sarah's Circle. They needed a food service coordinator. I found the address but it just didn't seem right. The neighborhood was really run-down. Homeless people were out on the sidewalk. Why would a restaurant be located here?

When I walked through the door, my jaw dropped. It was a large open space filled with hand-me-down chairs and couches. Artwork covered the walls, revealing images of pain, confusion and loss. The woman behind the desk asked me if I was there for an interview. I almost said "No" just so I could walk away. But "Yes" came out of my mouth.

I learned that Sarah's Circle is a day center for women who are homeless. They gave me a lot of statistics. Two out of every three homeless women have experienced a sexual assault. Getting a two-bedroom apartment in Chicago on minimum wage means you'd have to work 120 hours a week. There are well over 20,000 homeless individuals in Chicago.

And until that day, I'd only ever thought about feeding the rich.

I accepted the position and began a new journey in my life. I worked in the kitchen by myself and produced an average of 2,200 plates of food a month. The women weren't really interested in something fancy or something they didn't recognize. So that really challenged me. Thirty-five dollar plates were out of the question.

The money I had to work with was very limited. Most of my food came from the Greater Chicago Food Depository and the Anti-Hunger Foundation. Some stuff was pre-made. Pre-made and frozen. Like getting a bag of Arby's cheddar bacon sauce and trying to create a meal out of it. I didn't want to just thaw it out and serve it. I wanted to make it into something really wonderful.

I think Sarah's Circle made me a stronger chef. It was more than just cooking. It was therapeutic. To see a woman get a scoop of ice cream and say that she loves me and thanks God for it, was something I'd never experienced before. I was used to people complaining about the filet mignon.

It was like a 180-degree turn. Totally changed my perspective on what food is and why it's important. You got to eat. It's not always a luxury. Some people have to have food to live. And not because they have a hundred dollars to blow.

But you're not thinking about that when you're trying to be extra fancy. Details were the most important thing at my school. We only volunteered once, Thanksgiving. It was more about making as many turkeys as we could, as fast as we could, rather than the thought of where the turkeys were going. Didn't even seem like our volunteering was for the right reason.

I had to pick up a side job at a grocery store to pay the bills. I became the unofficial donation delivery driver. Sometimes I wouldn't get out of the grocery store until one in the morning and then I'd have to take donations to Sarah's Circle. I was exhausted. But I couldn't allow myself to see any food be thrown away. I'd become a homeless advocate.

And a year later I joined Inspiration. I knew Cafe Too is what I wanted to do. I supervise the internship in our restaurant, open for lunch two days a week. We're expanding to a full-service restaurant, open to the public seven days a week and run mainly by students through back-of-the-house and front-of-the-house training. When that opens, I'll be the chef.

Our classes average about fifteen students who are homeless, transient, underemployed or refugees. The curriculum is based on the Le Cordon Bleu Culinary School and it's packed full of information. Students are also trained in sanitation and safety.

After graduating, they receive additional services—meals, case management, art events and more. We help them get their resumes together, set up interviews, give job referrals and references. We do a thirty-day follow up, a sixty-day follow up, and a year follow up. It's great. They talk about their jobs. Some might come back to us and we'll keep placing them. We're a huge support system.

It's a really good feeling to teach people how to cook to become self-sufficient. Cooking is something everyone's done at least once, even if you were just making a peanut butter and jelly sandwich, you've cooked. It's a very simple skill—a lot of common sense and multi-tasking. And since everybody has to eat, it's a profession that's always going to be there.

Knowing how to cook for yourself is also very therapeutic—the nutritional side of it, the artistic side of it. It's great for someone that maybe has low self-esteem, feels like they don't have a skill. You get them in the kitchen. Show them a couple of easy tricks to make something beautiful. And it's amazing to see the self-accomplishment.

I think I'm pretty good at teaching. You really have to personalize. Different people work different ways, know different things. Breaking habits, that's huge. Your grandma taught you to do one thing. You did that your whole life.

And now I'm telling you it's wrong. That's really hard, like swallowing your pride sometimes. My students are usually twice my age and a different race and gender. Every three months I have to prove myself as an instructor.

I'm pretty strict when I teach. It's a tough field. You get yelled at a lot. You're on your feet all day. You could work an eleven-hour shift without a break. It's go, go, go, go. It's stressful. The customers, they expect everything perfect and fast. And that's how we have to give it to them. I'm not mean or anything, but I'm diligent. I try to pass that on.

I've had some students cry. For someone who maybe hasn't worked in a while, to come into this class and be expected to do a lot fast, it's overwhelming sometimes. But then they come back to me and they're like, "I'm glad you were tough with me. It helped me get to the position that I wanted. Helped me develop some leadership."

It's amazing. To be able to do that for just one person is awesome. But then to do that for like fifteen people every three months. You know? It's constantly rewarding. Every day.

I'm pushing out chefs left and right. And watching them graduate is very emotional. Their families are there, families that have supported them through thick and thin or families that have lost contact and then come back to see them achieve something. It's very beautiful.

Last summer, I stopped by Sullivan University where I graduated from culinary school. I saw the "success board" I used to walk by every single day. Pictures of Hawaiian resorts and cruise ships and graduates with great jobs. It's supposed to be motivating and inspirational.

I thought, "You know what? I'm successful now."

So I walked into the office and very bluntly said, "My name is Jenny Urban. I'm successful. I want to be on that board."

They kind of laughed at me. I started telling them what I did and how I got there. They were taken aback at first, but then they were moved. Nobody really goes through a year and a half of culinary school to work for the homeless.

My advice to future chefs is to see the whole picture. Food can be many things: an outlet, a means of bringing people together, an expression of art. But most of all, food is essential to live. It shouldn't be taken for granted, and neither should the ability to cook.

The skills that you develop in culinary school can take you many places. Allow yourself to share your talent with everyone because no one should ever go hungry.

Cuban Black Beans

Jenny Urban
Chef Trainer, Cafe Too

• • •

¼ cup olive oil

1 large onion, julienned

1 red bell pepper, diced small

¾ cup vegetable broth

2 tablespoons minced garlic

4 cans of black beans (2 cans drained and rinsed)

4 tablespoons cider vinegar

1 tablespoon brown sugar

1 teaspoon seasoned salt

2 tablespoons cumin

1 tablespoon onion powder

1 tablespoon paprika

1 teaspoon dried oregano

• • •

Sauté the onion, bell pepper and minced garlic in olive oil. Sauté until onion is translucent. Add the black beans and broth and bring to a simmer. Next add all remaining ingredients. While stirring with a wooden spoon, start to smash ¼ of the beans to get a thick consistency. Salt and pepper to taste.

Serves 4

A recent graduate of culinary school, Jenny Urban came to Chicago to work in the "mecca of fine dining." Unable to secure employment, she accepted a job serving meals at a day shelter for homeless women. The experience changed her as well as her ambitions. Today she is the chef trainer at Cafe Too. Every three months she graduates a new cohort of chefs.

Chapter Seven

COMPASSION

"Ten dollars in my hand."
Gloria Carter

"This is the one day I do something special."
Chris Brunn

"I want to feed the homeless."
Adie Martinez

"Just something that says I love you."
Mary Morgan

⋆ Creamy Pumpkin Soup ⋆
Chef Dominique Tougne

Gloria Carter

"Just to see that I helped one person makes it all worth it." Gloria squares her shoulders and straightens her back. Her white chef's jacket is stained from hours in the kitchen. "I spoke at a church on the West Side and this man came up to me. Told me he'd heard me speak before and it inspired him to come to Cafe Too." Her eyes catch mine. "He graduates this fall."

Heads nod knowingly around the table. Gloria lifts a spoonful of ice cream to her lips and smiles. "And I thought I was just wasting my time."

I had ten dollars in my hand and no one to turn to. The foundation of my family had been torn apart. I had nowhere to go. Just ten dollars in my hand. That's what they give you when you leave the penitentiary. Ten dollars and your bag in hand.

Staying in overnight shelters was really strange. I was born in Chicago but raised in the South by my great-grandmother. We had a nice home. Had a family. Always had nice things. So it gave me a reality check. This is what happens when you take the wrong route.

My great-grandmother, she gave me strong religious beliefs and principles. Instilled in me that I must get my education. And I did. Finished high school and continued on to college. But as I became older, I rebelled against her beliefs and what was taught to me.

I didn't want to go back to the West Side so I stayed on the South Side. But soon found myself around the same element of people I had before I went in. I tried to stay away but found it difficult. It was January. Cold outside. And I asked myself, "What am I going to do to make sure I don't go back?"

I started going to church. There was a church ministry open early in the morning, after we had to leave the shelters. And one morning sitting there it dawned on me that Genesis House always used to come out on the streets and talk to people.[1] So I asked around and someone told me where it was. I went there one morning and they took me in.

They said that drugs and prostitution was something I did. It wasn't who I was.

I never forgot that. Because I felt so bad, like what did I do wrong? Why does it keep haunting me? I paid my debt to society so why do I keep paying? I think I was better at beating myself up than society could ever do. I had to learn to forgive myself.

Genesis House taught me self-respect. How to love myself again. How to be a positive asset to society. They introduced me to Growing Home, an organic farming project, and the director told me about Cafe Too. He always knew that I love to cook.

So once he told me there was an opening, I was ecstatic. A couple of my sisters from Genesis House were inspired to follow my lead. All three of us graduated.

· · ·

It wasn't easy—meeting up at 4:30 a.m., getting on the buses and traveling out to LaSalle County to work this property—but it sure was better than anything on the street. The first week we went out, everything was flooded. And my first thought was, "How we supposed to farm?"

Well, Larry O'Toole, the farm manager, said, "Okay, it's trial and error here."

So we started laying out hay to absorb the water and the next thing you know, the weather dried up, the ground finally became dry enough and we started to plow. We started making seedlings in the greenhouses, just putting seeds in the earth and waiting for these little sprouts to come up. Broccoli, kale, Swiss chard, spinach.

I learned transplanting and cultivation and herb horticulture—and the terminology that you use. We had bees that we were extracting honey from. I loved the bee program. I learned to be a beekeeper. And then we'd go to different farmers markets. Hyde Park. Lincoln Park.

Once we sold our product, those funds went right back into the program, doing the same thing all over again. We made a stipend and the better we worked, the better our stipend was. Gave us an incentive to do the best work we could.

You'd be tired at the end of the day, but to see the end result was all worth it.

You get your hands in the dirt, like I used to do when I was a little girl growing up, weeding the garden with my great grandmother. Being in tune with nature was so tranquil. Not like the city, hearing all the sirens and troubles. You'd hear the tractor. Listen to the birds. See the squirrels.

And everything was organic. Whatever they take from the earth they put back to feed the earth. We made our own compost. No pesticides. No chemicals. No fertilizers. Because when you put those things into the earth, they kill the earth and hurt people, maybe not today but down the line. I learned that through them.

We planted all types of trees—apple trees, berry trees, weeping willow trees. Must have planted over seventy-five. Within the next thirty to forty years, they're going to be all these beautiful trees surrounding this farm, this farm that I have—we all have a part in. And one day, I'd like to tell my grandchildren about it. We'll ride out there and see the trees their grandmother planted.

It's like leaving your token on earth. I took them from when they were little branches and now they're like two or three feet high. Makes you feel good that you did something. They said the strawberries were running all over the place. And the raspberry bushes we planted—we didn't get much harvest off of them last year, but they say they're ready to go picking this year.

I'm just so grateful they're people out here that are trying to give people like myself a chance to change their lifestyle, to turn a negative into a positive.

• • •

I never went in for a violent crime. Everything was non-violent. Drugs. Prostitution. Hand-to-hand sale to a policeman. I never picked up a weapon. Never fought anyone. Not even when I was incarcerated. There's a lot of women in there like that. Non-violent crimes.

It's horrible. They treat you like animals. You're no longer a citizen. And you're in there with an element. Say someone gets a misdemeanor charge for possessing drugs or for selling their bodies, they find themselves right in there with people who've committed violent crimes, murder, rape, child molestation.

You become hardened. You may be scared but you become hardened. You have to. You don't want these people to jump on you or beat you or take advantage of you. And when you repress a person, they come out with less self-esteem than when they went in. They say, "What the hell am I fighting for? I don't have a chance."

So a person went in feeling bad and comes out feeling worse. What are the chances of them just pulling themselves up by their bootstraps? That's very difficult. And society doesn't make it easier. You go out looking for a job and because of your background, you're eliminated. It should be expunged. We made a mistake. We paid our debt. Why should we pay for forever?

I remember one inmate. Her name was Joanne. She always kept a smile on her face even though she was doing twenty-five years. She noticed I always kept to myself and one day she said to me, "Gloria, do the time but don't let the time do you."

I started going to school, continuing my college education. I worked in the kitchen. Did a lot of reading and a lot of listening to what other people were going through. I sat back and observed how some people were never going home and how blessed I was to know that one day those gates would open and I'd be leaving. I knew I didn't ever want to come back again.

So today I was out walking around, going from one SRO building to another, talking to people and letting them know there's an open forum on the governor's re-entry program for ex-offenders. We're trying to find strategies and suggestions on ways that people don't make incarceration a revolving door for themselves.

It's hosted by O.N.E.[2] They inspired me to come out and tell my story and how I've been trying to change my life. And I know there's people out there like myself that need help. I want to reach out. Do my part. I've taken from society and it's time for me to give back. To change some things that's in our society.

Incarceration isn't the answer. Thousands of women are in prison for non-violent crimes. They're away from their families, from society. At one time, I heard a state legislator say there was only a hundred women in jail. We're not building up society. We're tearing it apart. Tearing down the family structure.

And they're building more prisons. We have children who go to bed hungry every night, sleeping on the streets, selling their bodies. If we leave these kids out there with no parents and no one at home, what do we think that generation will continue to do with no guidance and no direction? We're just feeding it.

America, we really need to wake up. Maybe we should take a look at ourself in the mirror before we can tell somebody else how to run their country. We mistreat people here so. On a daily basis. And you know what they say, to end trouble, you nip it in the bud. Once it's grown out of control, it's kind of hard to get a grasp on it.

Sending a person back into society with no foundation and nowhere to go makes it very easy to turn to what's familiar. It's out there waiting for you at the gate. Soon as you step off that bus. But if we had more places like Genesis House and Growing Home and Cafe Too, these programs would greatly inspire people to change their lifestyles.

There are solutions. I mean, we can do something better than just locking people up and building more institutions to lock up more people. That's not working. Maybe instead of incarcerating people for non-violent crimes, we can make them do community service. Get out there and clean the streets. Work in the park districts. Plant flowers in the summertime. So they can say, "I've done community service. I have training. I can get a job."

The vast majority of us don't want to go back. We'd love to change what's happening but we just don't know how and we don't know where to go. So I think it's important, getting out there, knocking on doors and spreading the word that there's people out here, like myself, who are willing to work to do this. I don't get paid for this. And I'm not looking for pay.

There's a lot of people who inspire me to do something for myself and others. If they can come out—take the time that they could be enjoying their family—and help the homeless and the incarcerated and try to bring up our self-esteem, then I can do the same thing. Give back what was freely given to me. Give back to society.

• • •

I'm starting to bridge that gap with my family. Feels like a miracle. Sometimes I cry. It's been difficult and I'm sure they're still a little skeptical. But I'm talking to them again and they're talking to me. And I'm overjoyed.

I see my children have grown, coming into themselves as young men and young ladies. I'm a grandmother now. I have two grandchildren that I didn't know about before. And my son says how much I can be a grandmother to them. There was a time when he had hostility towards me and now he's open-minded and welcoming.

It's a great feeling. I can actually know them and they can know me. And not the old mom. I'm blessed. They're my blessing. They're gifts. I believe in the power of prayer. Prayer changes things.

And even though I don't understand a lot of things, I keep on believing and hoping that things can change, not just for myself but for others, too. I hate to see injustice in the world. To see others suffer, especially unnecessarily. To see people who've paid their debt to society come back and not be given a chance, a fair chance to do something different with their lives.

What a waste. There's a lot of intelligent people that are caught up in the penal system. They could be such assets to society. Maybe other people can read my story and find out they're not the only ones out there, not the only ones that have gone through struggles. Maybe they'll find ways to empower themselves, to change their lifestyle, to stop this vicious cycle.

And for other people who haven't had the struggle that I've had, maybe they can see the trials and tribulations that people like us—myself, the homeless, people who've been incarcerated, people who are trying to start over again—maybe they'll see what we go through.

• • •

Learning to forgive myself was a long hard struggle because even today I have a tendency to beat myself up. When things slow down or I run into another brick wall, I start to fall back, like boo-hoo, I'm trying so hard. And then it always seems like I hear someone going through more troubles than I am. Makes me smile and think, "Gloria, you're not the only one."

We're all out here going through a lot. Even people who are in the nine-to-five society. I learned that through my aunt. She's an executive nurse. Has two homes. I listen to her sometimes when I visit, and she says, "Oh, I have to put a new roof on the house…and the guys want to charge me…and I have to be at work…and my goddaughter left a grandbaby on me."

I'm not alone. I'm not exempt. And neither is anyone else. Everyone has something they're going through. And if not today, then maybe tomorrow.

You have to face life on life's terms. Do what you can. Do the best you can. Reach out for help and keep moving forward. Don't just sit there feeling sorry for yourself. Struggle is a part of life. Things are going to come your way.

Chris Brunn

"I've done volunteer work before, building houses. But the thing is when you're pound-ing shingles up on a roof somewhere, they really don't want you to be creative."

I laugh. Chris just smiles and sips his coffee. With his sandy-brown hair and thin face, you'd never guess he's thirty years old. He grew up in the suburbs and has been volunteering at the cafe for well over a year. An avid cyclist, he bikes there every Thursday morning.

"It's just a few miles. I don't know what it is exactly, but it gets me out of my usual routine, going downtown to work every day. This is the one day I do something special."

I remember the first time I stepped into the cafe. It was my first day to cook. Luke, another volunteer, hadn't gotten there yet and the kitchen was empty. Harry Madix, the cafe manager, said something like, "Okay, here's the kitch-en...." I remember pacing for like thirty minutes. I had no idea what to do. I'd never worked in a restaurant before.

I mean, here's this kitchen with stainless steel counter tops that go on forever, a big six-burner industrial stove, two ovens, a huge griddle, six or seven refrigerators and freezers. That's what really did it. All those refrigerators. I didn't know where anything was.

But I learned fast. Once we started cooking, it was really hectic. I don't actually remember the rest of the morning, but I felt like I made a significant difference. After a few weeks, I started coming up with my own segment of the menu. And now pretty much, for the past year and a half, I'm there every Thursday morning.

I had to do community service for a class I was taking. Went to a soup kitchen and ended up sleeping overnight. I remember being in the kitchen making peanut butter and jelly sandwiches with this guy. He was homeless. For some reason he'd got hooked up with the place and they gave him a job. He was just getting back on his feet. It was really cool to hear his story.

I mean, this is a guy who is just like anybody else. He lost his job and his girlfriend kicked him out. If only one of those happened, maybe he wouldn't be homeless. But he was. He'd just gotten a job out in the suburbs. He was waking up at like four in the morning to go out there. And here we are making peanut butter and jelly sandwiches for, I don't know, maybe fifty people.

I knew I wanted to volunteer again. And I knew I wanted to volunteer working with food. So I found the cafe. I remember meeting with Nancy Lee, the volunteer coordinator. It was kind of like going for a job, you know, but very informal. I wanted to cook vegan food. It's really, really important to me to eat compassionately and still have a good time.

Surprisingly, Nancy had no problems with it. I was thinking this is an established institution, you know, it's going to be a big deal to change. And it wasn't. I invaded with my vegan food. And now while the other volunteers are cooking up sausages and scrambled eggs, I'm doing my thing with vegan pancakes and French toast and a tofu scram.

I really like to cook and it's quite satisfying to do it at the cafe where people need a good meal. I want to go to culinary school or learn professionally in some other manner. I'm looking into that right now. Eventually I want to open up my own vegan cafe.

Last week, I brought a friend with me. I was so excited because this is something I love to do and now I can share it with one more person. As an activist, it's one of the things I get into. I have the desire to have a certain impact on the people around me.

The kitchen was pretty full. I went out front to serve. Finally got to meet the people I've been cooking for all this time. I know a name here and there, but now I'm getting to talk with them and learn more about them.

I still have to talk to them a lot more before I feel like I can really relate. But one thing that's becoming more and more clear to me is that I want to help people more generally in my life, to have a positive impact on what's happening around us, even if ever so small.

I try to look at the plates to see what people like, to see if they're eating all the food, or eating more of one thing than another, picking away a sauce or something.

But I don't usually see the plates coming back. The dishwasher's on the other side of the kitchen. So I have to work something out where we can communicate.

I know one guest is vegetarian. She really kicked off the tofu scram. More people started ordering it because of her. I know she really appreciated it. And maybe now that four of us are cooking, I can be out on the serving floor more, talking to people about how they like their food. It'd be interesting to see what comes out of that. And you know, maybe I'll mention that it's vegan. "How do you like it? Do you think it tastes the same?"

The thing about the cafe is it's so fresh. It has really cool murals on the walls. You've got these green hills rising, a farm scene, fresh vegetables, and the front of a tomato that just pops out at you. And then there are these pictures of different guests and alumni in the hallway as you walk in. It's a really vibrant place.

It's really incredible how the cafe provides meals to the guests in such a warm capacity. Just like a restaurant. You have the guests sitting down and the servers taking orders and bringing them coffee. We put up a menu and they can order whatever they want from it. We cook it straight away. It's all so personal.

We make the meal just for them, however they want it. We'll get orders for French toast plain. No powdered sugar, no dusted cocoa powder, no raspberries. And we won't put any on there. I mean, it's just for them. That's what's important. It's just the way they want it.

Adie Martinez

Adie is quiet. I hear our feet hitting the frozen pavement. I ask her why she's changed her mind about telling her story. Her deep-brown eyes look away at first.

"I've been homeless for three years and it has a way of making you doubt yourself. You stop taking risks. You lose your confidence. You become too afraid to trust. That's not me." She turns toward me. Her voice lowers. "I want to do this. I want to challenge myself to open up, to trust again."

Several months later, Adie stands before her fellow Cafe Too graduates. She looks like Aztec nobility; her thick waist-length hair sways against her back. "I want to feed the homeless," she tells the crowd. "That is my dream."

Being out on the street, the sidewalk is your pillow. You have no money. No food. No bed. You have nothing. Soap, shampoo, a toothbrush and toothpaste are luxuries. Salt and pepper, luxury. A hot shower, luxury. Tampax, luxury.

Homelessness crushes you. You feel like a crumb. I was so used to helping people and being there for them, but I couldn't. I had nothing to offer. I had no money, no food. I had time, but it was worth nothing. I felt like I was worth nothing. What could I give you?

Why would I give you my crummy time? You wouldn't want it.

• • •

Being homeless isn't about material things. You can live without them. To me, being homeless means having no support system. I wouldn't wish that on anybody. You need to have people who listen to you and tell you they care about you.

My daughter, my granddaughter and my therapist are my life. They're my strength. Nothing else matters to me as much as these three people do. It just seemed like overnight they were gone. Poof.

My daughter and granddaughter live with their aunt in California. I know they're really struggling, and that's hard for me. I pray for peace in that house.

It's easier for me to deal with my homelessness than it is for me to deal with their unhappiness.

I haven't seen my therapist in a long time either. She means the world to me. She's like my mother reincarnated. She gives me the strength to go on. And it saddens me to know that not everyone has someone like her. That is my wish for everyone, to have someone in their life who genuinely cares about them.

To me, time matters more than anything in the world. When someone gives me their time, that means more than a meal, and you know how much I love food. So that's why if somebody asks me to spend time with them, whether it's to teach them English or help them find directions, I try to be there.

Because if you can't find *one* person that you can rely on for that minute or that hour, it makes you wonder what you're here for. You know. And it's the same thing with the shelters. Some shelters are really good at spending time. Others let you know in a minute: This is just a place for you to stay, nothing else.

Some places are really, really strict about what time you come in and what time you leave. Feels like you're trapped. In one place the building was old and decrepit. You didn't even want to step foot in the shower. It was either use the bathroom in the dungeon—I called it the dungeon—or use the one up on the third floor. There weren't any curtains and the expressway was right there. It was so degrading, so demeaning.

We got kicked out. They have this rule that once you leave the shelter, you can't be on the premise. I thought we were far enough away, but I guess we were a couple feet too close. It was definitely a blessing. That's why I'm here at Marah's Place.

It was me and two other girls. One of the girls was pregnant. She ended up staying at Cook County Hospital because she thought she needed care and she didn't want to go to another shelter. The rest of us, we went to an emergency shelter. It was after dinner and we were hungry. They said we couldn't eat. They weren't serving meals at that time.

That place was really scary. They had bare light bulbs hanging on a string. Mattresses, maybe an inch thick, just like sleeping on the floor. The blankets were like the insulation you put underneath your carpet. They'd already been used by people who weren't clean. They were soiled with something or other. But when you're cold, you'll use it.

The next morning, the other girl that was with me woke up to a mouse nibbling at her hair. We were told to go downstairs to eat. The kitchen was filthy dirty. Roaches everywhere. They had these aluminum trays in the refrigerator and when they took the covers off, you couldn't even identify what it was. And they were going to feed it to us anyway.

That's when I just started crying. I left. I was hungry from the night before, but I knew I had to leave there. I knew it wasn't good for me. There had to be a better place.

I went to Catholic Charities and they told me about a drop-in center. I took a shower. Washed my hair. Washed the clothes I had on. Did some art work. I just felt so inspired by the women there. I was like, "Look at these women. They're in the same predicament I am and look at this lovely mural they've created."

The drop-in center told me about Marah's Place. They put my name on a waiting list. Told me I'd probably have to go back to the dungeon until something came open. Only this time, I really had to stay. I had to do as they said—which I did no matter how hard it was to take a shower in the dungeon or shower with no curtains or have my meals thrown at me.

I was pretty much being controlled there until something came open. And I just flew out of there. I was happy to never ever, ever, ever have to return. I'll sleep in the street before I go back there again. If I were to be homeless tomorrow, I wouldn't go there. I wouldn't go to the emergency shelter either. So at least I've learned some things. Now I know the good places from the bad places. Where to seek shelter and where not to.

At the next shelter, before I got into Marah's Place, I lived with a group of thirty women. It was a mixed population, and by that I mean, there were women with mental illness, extreme mental illness, prostitution, drug addictions, and then the general population. At times, we were subjected to really loud and ruthless women who had no respect for themselves, much less for other people.

We didn't really have a place where we could be alone. Everywhere we went there were people around. So I had to think of creative ways to find some sanctuary. I remembered the Park District. I used to go to the Field House. They had showers in the locker room.

And to keep up with my studies—I was majoring in culinary arts at Illinois Institute of Art—I'd buy a cup of coffee at Dunkin Donuts and just nurse it all day until my homework was done. Since I had to leave the shelter early in the morning and couldn't return until 7:30 at night, Dunkin Donuts gave me a place to be. I was able to keep a B average.

That's one thing: You do have choices. Being homeless, you may feel like you don't have any choices, but you *do*. You just have to be strong enough to think and have a clear mind about where you can go for help. Sometimes it's hard because they take decisions away from you. The ones they could take, they did. But the ones they didn't, it was up to me to either grin and bear it or not deal with it at all.

Don't come home at night. Or go somewhere else. On the days when I just didn't want to be there, I'd sleep in the street. Or I'd put myself down at Dunkin Donuts, get a cup of coffee, and just camp out. Whatever I had to do to survive. And, no matter how tough things get, I know I can always make my situation better or I can make my situation worse. I just have to deal with it the best way I know how.

Of course, being homeless feels better now. I have somewhere I can call home. I'm here at Marah's Place, where the people care about me and I care about them. I cried when I first opened my door. I could hardly turn the key in the lock. "Come on, Adie, open the door."

I couldn't stop crying. It was just that it…it was my room. My own room.

Marah's Place is an old convent. There are thirty or more women here. We have our own rooms. We share showers and we even have a bathtub on the main floor. We have a big kitchen so we all take turns in meal preparation and doing chores. We have a workout room in the basement. We have a TV and laundry facilities. It's really terrific.

They offer job and employment assistance. They help with tutoring, art therapy and scholarships. They helped me with my books and tuition. When my scholarship money ran out at Illinois Institute of Art, they told me about Cafe Too. I'm really happy to be here.

We're pretty much on our own. They're here for you, but they don't invade your privacy. They don't demand of your time. Their hours are generous. We can stay out 'til midnight, whereas in the shelters, our curfew was 7:30 p.m. If we had anything that we had to do at night, we couldn't because we'd lose our bed.

But even now, I have to ask myself, "What's going to help me get through all of this until I get my own place? Until I get my full-time job?" No more of these part-time jobs here and there. What's going to make me stronger? What's going to help me stand on my own two feet? By myself. Without my therapist. Without my daughter. Without my granddaughter.

Physical activity makes me stronger. Being able to shoot hoops or go for a run. Being able to lift heavy things without anybody's help. Being able to hold back when I just really want to throw a fit and be angry. Being able to hold on until I can get to a place where I can just let loose and cry my eyes out. Not everybody knows how to handle that.

That's why I'm really careful. Who touches me, who doesn't touch me. Who talks to me, who doesn't talk to me. Who helps me, who doesn't help me. I'm extremely careful with myself.

Call it snobbiness. Call it arrogance. I don't see myself as arrogant or vain or snobby. I see myself as someone who is really selective because I don't want to get hurt. It's taken a lot for me to get to where I am. And I consider these choices that I can make now.

I try to find ways to uplift myself, like this bracelet I got for a dollar at Walgreens. I like to think up things that will inspire me. Besides physical activity, there are truffles, chocolate truffles. They just really excite me to no end. And there are places I love to go and just enjoy the silence.

And oh, do I have something really special to share with you. I finally did the one thing that I've been dying to do, that I didn't think I could do, so I wouldn't even try.

I got these little rubber stoppers for my bed so it won't roll away from the wall.

And I got in the tripod position—I don't know if you ever took gymnastics but I remembered that from gym class—but my arms are so bony, my knees wouldn't stay on my elbows. They just kept wobbling off.

And no matter how many times I fell over, I just kept talking myself into trying harder and harder. "Come on. You know you can do it. Get up there and try again."

And somehow, I finagled my way up. The rest is history. I actually did a headstand on my bed. And I'm a tall woman, okay? It just took a lot of courage and strength. I felt so incredibly special. Beyond special. There is no word for it. It was euphoria. Total euphoria. I screamed into my bed, "I did it. I did it."

I do stuff like that to keep myself in high spirits. Sometimes I make a list of what's going to make me happy. Or I look to see what needs to be done or who needs help. I try different things. And when I don't have to go to school or go to work, it's like, "I'm not going to do a damn thing." Sometimes it just feels good to sit and ponder.

I'm really happy to be where I am, at Marah's Place and in Cafe Too. I want to learn everything there is to know about feeding the homeless. I want to experience all the aspects of a restaurant because I don't know the behind-the-scenes in the kitchen enough to really have my own restaurant yet or to be a chef for that matter.

But I do know that feeding the homeless entails a lot more than just handing out a meal. I want to interact with the people who've been out there like I have. I want to hear their story, to lend a hand, to be there if they just want to cry on my shoulder. Or if they just want me to listen.

Sometimes that was more important than the meal. Just to have a warm hand to hold or somebody to listen. Somebody to tell me that they genuinely cared.

I hope and pray I can pursue my dream with Cafe Too. I really care about what they're about. It's my way of giving back to the community. And being that I grew up in Uptown, it's really close and dear to my heart. I just can't think of a better way to say "I love you" to somebody in need than with a meal, and maybe a smile and a hug.

Mary Morgan

Ms. Morgan, as she's most often called, is wearing a purple dress. Its richness high-lights the deep tones in her face. But for a touch of gray by her temples, you'd never know she's almost sixty years old.

We sit side by side, huddled over the tape recorder in a small office cubicle less than five feet from the kitchen and dining area. The Living Room Cafe is full, and I have to lean in to hear her soft voice. She tells her story without interruption, pausing only to catch her breath.

Weeks later I tell her I have written her story. "Oh, how does it sound? Is it all right?" she asks me. We sit side by side in the same tiny office cubicle and she reads it to herself. By the last page, she is rubbing my back. "You understand," she whispers. "You understand."

I've been coming for a little over four years. The Living Room Cafe is a wonderful place. I feel it within my heart. I'll tell you about Laura.[3] She taught me about every time I get my check.

She said, "Mary, take some money and write down a list of what you want. Write down what you need and what you don't need. But remember you have to travel. Get you a bus pass. Buy your food. Get your clothes out of the cleaners. Then see what you have left. Put it aside. Put it in the bank. Go buy you a little outfit but don't buy a whole lot of outfits. Just get one."

Laura told me that. She really helped me and she made me really proud. I gave her a black dress and she wore it. See I can manage off my income. It may not be much. I pay cheap rent. Don't have to pay no electric or gas. Pay light.

. . .

In a whisper that sounds like poetry, she says:

The Living Room Cafe,
it's something to do,
somebody to talk to,
somebody to smile when you smile,
somebody to laugh when you laugh,
somebody to help when you need help,
not only help,
but help with a feeling,
a kind word,
something to say,
something to ask,
just something that say
I love you.

• • •

I don't want someone to make the mistakes I made in the past. When I was growing up, things was kind of rough. The reason why I say rough is because you don't find too many fathers that will abuse their own child. I was taking care of the young kids and my mama didn't know what my father was doing to me in the basement. I was a teenager. I didn't know. And it be a problem because I had to tell somebody, and the person I told, they didn't believe me.

My father, he got a divorce from my mother and brought me to Chicago. My second mother took care of me just like a mother would take care of a child. And my grandmother told me how to keep myself clean and not to bother with boys at the present time. She let me go to church. I got filled with the Holy Ghost.

But, my second mother passed away. Died of cancer. My father remarried. The third wife, she put him out. Things wasn't how they suppose to be. She thought he had money and would care for her kids and her family. When I was put out, I didn't have no place to go.

Went to my sister's house. She was glad to have me, long as I obey her rules and regulations, not to go out and stay out all night long, doing things I'm not suppose to do. They was trying to help me find a job. My sister's tenant asked me to be with his wife and clean house. That's what I was in the field of doing, cleaning house.

She was a nice old lady. And I loved her. I know deep down in her heart wherever she is right now, she know I didn't mean to take it. I didn't mean to take her money. I needed money at that time. Times was hard. But she was good to me.

After that, everything began to get bad again. I left there and went to the South Side. Managed to go into a nursing home where people would get little odd jobs and manage their bills. I worked for a lady. She was in the paper. She was taking money from the government. She got put in jail.

I went over to another place on the North Side, Wilson Avenue, where I did labor work. I was trying to keep in touch with my dad. I still needed some comfort, not sexually wise. Didn't have feelings for that. I was a straight-up woman. Wanted a husband. I'd meet different men that I liked, going out, parties and things like that. My father would come by and see me. That place, it was a mess. They closed the place up. My father took me back in.

Then for a while, I was just staying in different hospitals, Mantino, Tinley Park, Jackson Park. So many hospitals. I just was sick of it. I asked the Lord to give to me a way where I be safe and comfortable. Managed to get another job working on the South Side. I tried to keep jobs, something to keep my head steady so I wouldn't have to go back to being sick again.

My husband, he took good care of me. He saw me and he loved me. I saw him and I loved him. We worked together. He may have had bad days and everything, but we understood one another, our feelings, our actions, everything.

I just didn't like getting sick. It's a bad feeling. Couldn't take care of my babies. Had to give them up because of necessity. He thought I was crazy. He said, "You mean to tell me you give up your babies?"

I said, "I have to give them up because you drinking and I can't take you drinking if I have them too." It was all right when we was together, but when we started having babies, that's when it was hard. He had to let me go. He say, "You going to be well taken care of baby. Just be careful. Don't do nothing that you may hurt yourself in doing." He told me, "I'll be back."

So now, everywhere I go, no matter, I know I have to take those pills when I get to shaking. Have to take them pills to stay steady. I'm not like I used to be. Can't act like no child. I'm a grown woman. When I see that I get sick and I can just take so much, I go in my little corner and talk to my God. I say, "Lord, help me. I know not what I do. Make me better."

I may cry sometimes. I ain't cried in a long time. Only when I think about my husband. His memory is still there if I play it.

• • •

The Living Room Cafe,
it's something to do,
somebody to talk to,
somebody to smile when you smile,
somebody to laugh when you laugh,
somebody to help when you need help,
not only help,
but help with a feeling,
a kind word,
something to say,
something to ask,
just something that say
I love you.

• • •

The Lord brought me a long ways. Going to church was my obligation. I wanted to learn about him. He helped me. Keeps me in the frame of mind that I can't turn away from him. If I do something wrong, I know I've done him wrong and I have to tell him I'm sorry. I don't want to be like that. I ask for his mercy.

One day, when that day comes, he's going to say to me. "If you going to be accepted in my kingdom, you got to do right before you come up." That's the way I feel. My God knows best. Peaceful God. Merciful God.

Couldn't take care of my babies. I take care of them now. Send them what I can. I just pray that one day my little girl will let me see her when she come in town some time this year. I've been praying for it a long time. See my baby. See my son too.

Haven't seen them since they was grown. They been constant working at different places, but I manage to see they godmother who took them, the foster parents that receive my grandbabies. I was so happy. Had to pay sixty dollars. I sacrificed that sixty dollars. Next time, I asked the man would he take me again to see my grandbabies. He said he will.

I used to worry about my daddy. Bother me. Talking to me and telling me this and that. I told him to pray. He's up in heaven and I'm down here now. I don't want someone to make the mistakes I made in the past. My daddy abused me. You got a child, a girl child, watch out. Tell the little girls to watch out. They got a whole life ahead of them.

· · ·

The Living Room Cafe,
it's something to do,
somebody to talk to,
 somebody to smile when you smile,
somebody to laugh when you laugh,
somebody to help when you need help,
not only help,
but help with a feeling,
a kind word,
something to say,
something to ask,
just something that say
I love you.

Creamy Pumpkin Soup

Dominique Tougne
Executive Chef, Bistro 110

• • •

1   large pumpkin, 10 pounds
1   gallon water
2   pounds unsalted butter
1   quart heavy cream
    salt and pepper to taste

• • •

Peel the pumpkin. Remove the seeds. Cut the pumpkin meat in small pieces, 2" x 2". In a large pot, display the cut pumpkin. It should represent ⅔ of the pot. Add the water to cover the pumpkin. Season with salt and pepper.

Cover the pot and cook over medium heat until the pumpkin is soft. Strain half of the liquid and keep aside. With a hand-mixer, purée the pumpkin until very smooth. If it is too thick, add some of the cooking liquid back in. Otherwise, discard extra liquid.

Cut the butter in small dices. Keep the soup on the stove over low to medium heat. With a hand-mixer, add the butter in small quantities. Then add the heavy cream. The soup should have the consistency of clam chowder. Season to taste and garnish with sautéed mushrooms, roasted scallops or sun-dried tomatoes, if desired.

Serves 8-10

Dominique Tougne is a member of the board of directors for Inspiration Corporation. He has been volunteering, planning and preparing the Anniversary Dinner, Inspiration's annual fall fundraiser, for several years. Each Anniversary Dinner is a multi-course extravaganza.

Considered a protégé of leading chefs in France, Dominique came to the States with two suitcases, one hundred dollars in his pocket and no work permit. He landed at Bistro 110 and has been the executive chef since 1996. To him, cooking is about "Sharing with people you love."

Chapter Eight

⇥ TRUST ⇤

"Tears of joy."
Gerald Holman

"The days go fast."
Phil Green

"We have to aspire to greatness."
Erick Hampton

⇥ Inspiration Cafe Wednesday Morning Tortilla Casserole ⇤
Michael Kuhn

Gerald Holman

Gerald always comes into the cafe on Friday mornings with Starbucks coffee. I love to tease him. "What?" I say. "Our coffee isn't good enough for you?" And then we both laugh. I don't even drink coffee so how would I know?

This morning, we talk for several hours. He's thirty-five. He serves on the board of a local social service agency, and he volunteers through his church to help young children with their schoolwork. Gerald was on the streets for fifteen years.

He wears a silver chain with a cross and a gold wedding band. His eyes are gentle, his head shaved, and his voice soft and low. He told me once, "I'm kinda a softie, you know. I cry easy. And, I generally want to care for people."

My grandmother, she gave me my religious upbringing. Provided for me—things for school, moral values, a bigger outlook on the world. She used to take me and my younger sister and brother to see the boats on Lake Michigan. She'd take our picture in front of them.

One of my greatest memories is when she'd supposedly take us to see the fireworks. It would always be the wrong day, so she'd take us to see the orchestra play instead. I'd always cry, "Where's the fireworks?"

It's just so amazing—being married now for three years I see a lot of my grandmother come out. I never thought I'd be interested in the arts. My wife, she's interested in arts. We go to jazz concerts. See ballet dances. Listen to classical music. And I tear.

It ain't tears of sorrow, like it was when I was little, but tears of joy and happiness for things that I'm able to experience today after going through what I've gone through, between the time when I was growing up with my grandmother and where I am now. I think it's just tears of gratitude that I've been given a second life.

I remember just recently, I was talking to my mother. We're either laughing or we're yelling at each other. But this time when she called—we'd apologized as we usually do—she told me, "Gerald, I'm really proud of you for all that you've accomplished. Working at Starbucks. Getting married…."

And I was like, "Okay."

I didn't let her know how it really impacted me. I started crying. It felt like something had lifted off of me. I didn't know I was carrying such a big weight. All my life I used to always try to distance myself from everything that affected me in a negative way. And her saying that proved to me that…that those very things are the things I had to make peace with.

Telling my story means I have a chance to acknowledge my past as well as my present, to accept them as equal, and to not deny myself the same hopes and dreams that others have. I've learned that you get just as much confidence cleaning up a mistake as the person being promoted or doing something good. You're both going in the same direction. Ain't that something?

• • •

We bounced between my grandmother and my mother. With my mother, we went from house to house. We were always sent in the back room. She'd stay up front and party and dance.

But the party always ended up in an argument with these so-called male friends. And she'd wake us up at like three or four in the morning. She'd be yelling at us, expecting us to feel the…the urgency to leave as she did. It really hurt us.

So, growing up in that environment, we had no self-esteem. Thought we didn't measure up. I wanted to please everyone so I started living a double life. Joined a gang. Graduated valedictorian from high school.

I wanted everybody to say, "That's good, Gerald." But not everyone would. Some people would say it. I'd always get some people. But others would say, "Oh, you ain't nothing."

I started drinking. Smoking marijuana. I was sixteen. Later I moved on to heavier drugs. I knew it wasn't right. See, my grandmother—that part of me said this is morally not right. I wanted to escape. But then that other part said, "You're nothing. There's nothing you can do."

Once I started doing crack, I dropped off the slope fast. I began to do illegal things. Sold fake drugs to get real drugs. Panhandled. Male prostitution. I had an addiction that was out of control. And this went on for like fifteen years of my life.

I distanced myself from my family. When people asked me about my parents—they'd say, "Wow, you too young to be out here." And I'd tell them my family was dead. After a while seemed like I believed it. My family was dead to me.

I just wanted to be free. To break free from my mother. Make my own decisions. But I hadn't grown up, so the decisions I made were really immature. I wasn't ready to be free. But that was the biggest thing I wanted. To be free as a bird. No one could tell me anything.

I could do anything I wanted to do. And so what did I want to do? I wanted to feel good. What made me feel good? Alcohol. Drugs. Sex. Anything that made me feel good, I did.

But all those same fears and anxieties I had growing up—what I called "my enslavement"—I carried with me. They directed my course. And I didn't even realize it. When I was out there, I was still enslaved. I thought if I was free, it'd be different.

When I finally came to realize that, I wanted to be free again. But this time with the freedom, I wanted peace.

• • •

The second time I got sober I was thirty-one. This time I wasn't so much focused on the drink or the drug. I was focused on the emptiness, the need for forgiveness, my own and the divine.

The first time, I was sober for two years. I obtained a job working for Wally's Hamburgers. Worked my way up to assistant manager. Got into a housing program. But I stopped working the programs. Stopped working with the cafe. And I became lonely. Felt like there was some empty hole in me that had begun to be filled. I went back out there.

It seems like my greatest pain comes from loneliness. And it's not loneliness of not being around people. I can be around people and still feel the loneliness. It's like I used to always ask, "Why am I here?" Having been sober and then gone back out on the streets, my path was a broken path.

But I finally came to realize that that broken path had been blessed. All the coincidences in my life wouldn't have happened if there wasn't a divine power that had blessed that broken path for me. And that allowed me to make peace with my past.

And, it gave me hope that the road ahead of me was…was…there was a road ahead of me that was prepared whether I knew it or not. That's the hope I live in today. That's the hope that keeps me strong today. That's my foundation.

I learned that I could find peace within me. In any disturbance, I can find peace within. And you know what? That was freedom, freedom from my thoughts. Knowing that what I was searching for, that God would give me what I needed, even when I really didn't know what that was.

Sometimes, you know, I'm not comfortable with what's going on in my life. I can't say I'm always happy. I can't say I'm always grateful. But you know what? I have a joy. I have a joy today that everything is right where it should be at this very moment.

I used to wonder how people could be so calm and peaceful. And then I noticed that sometimes I am relaxed. My muscles are relaxed, and so much is going on. So I'm like, "Wow." There's this joy that you can have, no matter what's happening.

• • •

I got hired at Starbucks. I didn't want no job. All I wanted to do was go to Emmaus Ministries every day.[1] Go to bible study. But one day I was walking by Starbucks, and they were having an open house. So I went in just for fun. I was busy talking and stuff, and they said, "We want to offer you a job."

I was like, "What?" This wasn't supposed to happen. Was it God?

So I started working at Starbucks. And you know what I did? I started bragging, you know, like look at me now. And this woman I'd been with for eight years, she gave me an ultimatum. Spend more time with her or stick with God and Emmaus Ministries. I chose God. She left. I didn't show up for work.

After a couple of months, the loneliness brought me back. Everyone at Emmaus Ministries convinced me to go back to Starbucks. At first I said, "No." Pride. I wouldn't even walk that way.

And there was never one time in my life when I couldn't get a job. But I could not get a job. So I finally stopped in and talked to the manager. He offered me my job back. He said, "You'll never be able to be promoted with this company again. You'll stay a barista." They knew about my background. They knew why I had left.

I said, "Okay." I was so happy. It didn't matter.

And God say, "Look where you are now. You don't care about the job label. You just have gratitude for just being where you are."

So I was working hard as ever and I made a promise to God. I'm not going to look for companionship. I don't want anything except our relationship. The next thing I know, the district manager was changed. The new manager promoted me to shift supervisor. He knew me from Wally's Hamburgers.

I said, "God, I just don't understand."

And God say, "Just keep on."

Then one night I was sitting and taking a break, reading my bible and somebody say, "Gerald, look up." I looked up and this young lady—our eyes caught and we stared at each other the whole time she walked past the store.

This happened every night. I'd take a break at the same time and I'd be watching the windows. Where is she? Then one night, she just came in. I was so shy. She seemed sort of god-like. She had an aura about her and it was unlike any other person.

I found out she's a Christian. She works at the Moody Bible Institute. She'd never been in a coffee shop before. She doesn't even like coffee. She's so not me. I love coffee. I come home smelling like coffee. Only now I know she is so me.

A year later we were married. We've been married three wonderful years. Well, the first year was really troublesome. It was like on the edge. As if we had to start all over again, get to know each other, make peace with our true selves, who we really are. And you know what? Accepting our true selves, now we see how we fit more than ever.

She's going after her degree. And me, I'm going to follow the passion of my heart. And that passion has led me to now—after being with Starbucks since 1999, I gave a one month notice after applying to Cafe Too. I didn't know if I was going to get the job. I went on the experience that I had with God previously. I felt a piece of me say, "Do it now. Trust."

So I did. And after a while, when I didn't hear anything, I said, "Okay God, you're not…."

And God say, "Are you going to trust me even when you're not sure?"

Two weeks later I was offered the position. Shift lead barista at the new restaurant. Same position I had at Starbucks, supervising the other baristas. Only now, I can mentor those coming through the Cafe Too program.

So now I understand what a spiritual leader is. Follow him. Trust him. God will expand your life. Sometimes, I'm like, "You still listening God?"

He say, "Yes I am. Only now, you're trusting in that. I don't have to chase after you to prove it to you. You're trusting in that faith."

The only time I really feel that faith is when I look back over my life. I went through a struggle and God brought me through it. And now, there's a peace. It's like he's saying, "Gerald, it's okay."

"You sure?"

And God say, "There's two sides to this. Go with me first. I got it."

I just have to remember that I don't know everything. I can't see the whole picture. And no matter what kind of storm you're going through, there's no way one individual can see the whole picture.

So I try to keep an open mind to a message that might be near. It can come through anything. Through a person. Something you read. An experience. Something in your past. You just got to take some time out to listen. It's only a moment out of your life but it could make a world of difference.

Now, I just take the steps. I say, "What's next? What's the next right thing for me to do?" And I turn the rest over to God. I may see the worst possible scenario but I don't let it direct me, or put me in such a state of fear that I'm paralyzed. I don't let anything paralyze me.

· · ·

I like to read motivational books, spiritual books. And when I read them, they're not telling me what I should do, they're telling me that what I've learned to believe is true. Some things I read, I'm like, "Yes. I've been there." You know that sense of "Yes, that's me."

I used to always use the word "coincidence," and I think that's my sense of spirituality. And you know what? I get a sense of spirituality in the cafe. I may come in thinking I'm not going to talk to anyone, and the next thing I know somebody talking about sports, or whatever, and I'm like, "Yes." There's a connection. A bond.

That's my vision for Cafe Too. Bonding. Spirituality is bonding, bonding with others and bonding with God. And when you're bonding with others, it's just the icing on the cake that tells you everything is just not aimlessly happening.

I'm constantly getting that feeling that this is not aimlessly happening.

Phil Green

"The days go fast," he says. "Trust me." Phil rolls down his window. The trees outside are in full bloom. My hands rest on the steering wheel.

I know he's dying. Pancreatic cancer has eaten away half his body weight. His skin is ashen. "The doctor say, can't do nothing. Just make me comfortable, you know." He smiles weakly as if trying to somehow make the conversation easier. My heart aches.

"Are you scared?" I ask.

"I ain't scared," he replies. "Apprehensive." The light turns green. "Curious, you know?"

He cracks a smile and starts to tell me about his music. How he still composes late at night. How the flute, sax, vocals were once his life….

In the months before he died, Phil was reunited with former bandmates and childhood friends. They hadn't heard from him in over twenty years. Many assumed he was already dead. At his memorial service this past fall, they described Phil in the exact same ways we knew him. Spirited. Lively. Honest. A man who could talk to anyone. And a man who always did.

Phil's picture hangs above the welcome table at Inspiration Cafe. I pause there from time to time. I miss him. He used to sing lyrics from old love songs while we sat waiting for his breakfast. I'm sure I'm not the only person he sang to. The memory of it heartens me. It's good to know that life doesn't have to change the essence of who we are or how we choose to live.

• • •

Phillip Green
February 22, 1943–November 21, 2005

Erick Hampton

Spread across the table are snapshots of his artistic work: playbills from The Cuentos Foundation and Scrap Metal Soul, an Uptown acting troupe.[2] Published poems from the Journal of Ordinary Thought.[3] *Headshots. Drafts of an original play. Stage manager directions for an upcoming performance.*

"Everything is just taking off," Erick's smile widens. "It's like the old song goes: The future's so bright, I'm going to be blinded by the light!"

A hearty belly laugh fills the room. As I write his words, they fall naturally into verse.

I.

I'm proud to be sharing my story with other folks.
It's a story that needs to be told.

I was going to school full-time,
majoring in English and communication,
and working forty hours a week.
But couldn't maintain the schedule,
so I left my job.

It was my third time in college.
Three times a charm, you know.

I was getting good grades.
Was well-liked.
Was just finishing a play.

Nobody asks.

When you're on the street,
nobody asks you.

"Where do you come from?"

"What are you all about?"
"How did you become homeless?"
"What's it like being this way?"
It's like a burden you're holding within you.

I didn't want people to look at me differently,
but they seemed to.

Thought I was doing everything right.
　　Probably should have kept my job.
Thought I'd find another job quickly.
　　But it didn't turn out to be that way.

My money started running out.
　　Poor spending habits.
I was getting good grades.
　　But wasn't getting any jobs.

Had to give up the place I was living at.
　　I became homeless.
　　　　I was twenty-eight.

Homelessness isn't limited to certain groups.
　　It's not just black people, like myself,
　　not just older people
　　not just people from the inner-city
　　not just people who suffer from mental illness.

We have white folks who are homeless
　　people from the suburbs who are homeless
　　people who were doing pretty good,
　　people who
　　　　　　ran companies
　　　　　　were managers

                                    had big positions
                   people who went to good schools.

                   It hits everybody.

                   Nobody is immune to homelessness.
                   Nobody.

Friend of mine told me to check out the cafe.

   "Don't want to.
      Too busy."

Finally went to a job fair at Truman College.
Met two beautiful ladies,
   Margaret Haywood and Rian Wanstreet.
They encouraged me to check out Cafe Too.

   "Why not?"

Graduated September 27, 2002.
Worked for the cafe.
   They helped me find other jobs.

I've been working my way up ever since,
   almost three straight years.
Working for a catering company now.
   Love it.
   Really do.

II.
Being homeless was an adventure.
   It was wild.
      Freaky.
Anything you can imagine it to be,

it was.

Being out in these streets was sometimes,
    just very, very sad,
       mentally trying,
       trudging around from day to day,
       getting turned down for the job interview,
         not having enough money,
           lack of sleep,
             sometimes threats,
             even on your life,
               sleeping with one eye open.

It started setting me up, you know.
    I felt myself slipping away.

               I come from such a good background.
               Why would this happen to me?
               Not Erick.
               Not me.
               I was in school.
               I was working.
               I had a place.
               And now I'm living in a shelter?

               My mom would be ashamed.

Never wanted for anything growing up.
    Was always fed.
    Dressed really well.
I was pushed to be the best that I could be.
    And that's what I became.
God bless Priscilla Elaine Cole Horn.

She loved me, my brother, my sister.

    Couldn't have asked for a better foster mom.

So the shelter system was totally new for me.

    Didn't know how to find them.

    Didn't know how to live in them.

    Had my own ideas about who stayed in them.

But all that shattered once I started talking to folks.

They were actually very nice people.

    Came from different walks of life.

    Did pretty amazing things

    before they were homeless.

    It was an eye-opening experience.

Those folks kept me from crumbling.

    They really gave me hope.

            It's not just all about me.

            They've suffered too.

                They've been down,

                and they're working themselves up.

            This is where I'm at.

              But not where I'm going to end up.

They were my beacon of light, what kept me strong,

    'til I got my own place.

III.

I believe if you keep your hope up,

    your mind straight,

    your faith in something.

        be it your religious faith

the strength of your past
the love of your family and friends
anything that you can hold onto
that inspiration will carry you out.

That's what I did.

I'd go to Gary, Indiana from the city,
and my nieces and nephews
would jump all over me and tackle me.
I'd go falling down,
laughing and laughing.

They'd look so sad to see me go.
Just made me feel really good.

Erick,
You are somebody.
You came from somewhere.
You do have what it takes.
You are not what people say you are.
You are what you want to be.

I drew upon my faith in God.
Cannot say that enough.
My love for Jesus, his love for me,
that's what saw me through this.
It was just him
teaching me.

"This is a stepping stone.
A learning experience.
Go through this and share it with others,
and I will reward you in kind.

Stay faithful.

Great things are coming to you in the future."

Some days I went to the library.

Did a lot of reading when I was homeless.

Oprah Winfrey

Malcolm X

Jesse Jackson

Martin Luther King

People who lived in bad times and rose above it.

Reading those positive, encouraging words,

made me hold my head up high.

I am more than what I think I am.

I can aspire to greatness.

Sometimes I'd go into the shelter and just be beaming with light.

"How's it going Erick?"

"I'm doing great, man.

I'm on fire."

A lot of people were sad to see me go.

I always knew this was going to be temporary.

Was bound to do better things.

I was always trying to search myself.

Who am I?

I am a lover of life.

I am a beloved uncle.

I am a damn good actor.

I am an aspiring poet and writer.

I am a great singer.

I am a lover of people.

We have to aspire to greatness.
   We have to know who we are.

People might think lowly of us,
   just because we're in this situation.
We can't let how they feel hold us down.

IV.

And now,
right now is so good,
I can hardly contain myself!

I'm with Scrap Metal Soul,
   an acting troupe in Uptown.[4]
They get people from different walks of life,
   put them into this one body of creative force,
   and let them do their thing,
      whether it's acting, singing, dancing, playing music.…

People are moved.
   Lives are changed.

People saw the powerful piece I did for the spring show.
   "Invisible."

Afterwards the head of Scrap Metal Soul asked me,
   "Would you like to help us with writing some scripts?"

      "Why, sure I would."

A woman from the Cuentos Foundation saw "Invisible,"
   wanted me to be in an ethnographic piece, "Breaking Bread."

   Standing room only.

It's just been a total 360°.

A total 720°.
A double turnaround.

I owe this all to my Lord Savior,
to growing up, knowing who I am,
and surrounding myself with uplifting people,
actually thriving off of people like you—
very positive, warm, giving, sincere.

It's just like I said,
"The future's so bright,
I'm going to be blinded by the light!"

So, look out for me
'cause I'm coming.
I'm coming strong.
Erick Hampton is coming soon.

He's gonna take Chicago by storm…
and then the world!

So stay tuned for more.…

the best is yet to come.

Inspiration Cafe Wednesday Morning Tortilla Casserole

Michael Kuhn
Private Chef

• • •

16	ounces good quality tortilla chips
16	ounces salsa, heat depending on taste
1	cup water
1	medium onion, minced
4	tablespoons olive oil
¾	cup cooked black beans
¾	cup corn kernels
	salt and pepper to taste

Optional for garnish: chopped cilantro, sour cream, grated cheddar cheese, thinly sliced green onion

• • •

Generously grease a 9" x 12" casserole dish. Sauté onions in olive oil until soft and translucent. Add salsa, water, corn and black beans. Bring to simmer. Put chips in a large heat-proof bowl. Pour salsa mixture over chips. Stir lightly to coat all chips. Cover and let steam for 10 minutes. Put in casserole dish. Bake at 350 degrees, uncovered for 15 minutes. If desired, sprinkle with cheddar cheese and return to oven for 5 minutes or until cheese is melted.

Serve for brunch with scrambled eggs or use to accompany roasted chicken or grilled fish. If desired, sprinkle the plate with chopped cilantro, green onion and sour cream.

Serves 4

Michael Kuhn started cooking breakfast at Inspiration Cafe in 1999 and he's been on the board of directors ever since. "I cook a lot for people who want my cooking," he tells me. "But here, people need my cooking. It gives me a reason to get out of bed. I feel more dignity and respect when I'm offering dignity and respect to others."

You can still find Michael at Inspiration Cafe on Wednesday mornings. His tortilla casserole is a favorite of guests, alumni, staff and volunteers.

Afterword

If addiction were the sole cause of homelessness, half of Hollywood and half of all professional athletes would be homeless. But they're not. They don't live in poverty.

– Christopher Persons
Executive Director, Inspiration Corporation

• • •

More than thirty million people in the United States live in poverty. The poverty line for a family of three is $12,750; for a family of four, $16,813. Homelessness is poverty at its worst. Men and women who are homeless are the poorest of the poor.[1]

Sociologists identify two types of causes that put people at risk for homelessness. Proximate causes are issues linked to individuals—mental illness, family crises, financial strain, addiction or disjointed work histories—while ultimate causes are linked to larger systemic issues: national employment policies, affordable housing, access to health care and quality education, and ever increasing poverty.

In the 1980s, the gap between the housed and the unhoused grew exponentially. Between 1973 and 1993, over one million SRO units were demolished and 2.2 million low-rent units disappeared from the market. The average wait for public housing vouchers is now thirty-five months.

Recent surveys in major cities reveal that almost a quarter of all homeless men and women work. But in every state, a full-time minimum wage job proves to be insufficient for a family to pay fair market rent for a two-bedroom apartment.

• • •

Sociologists also identify three types of homelessness. A single experience of homelessness is different from episodic homelessness, or cycling in and out of being homeless. Many of these men and women we pass on the street, without even realizing the reality of their living situations.[2] But the men and women who become homeless and appear to remain homeless—what sociologists term chronic homelessness—are more readily identifiable. We see them every day. They are the most visible.

Current policy and advocacy work, including Chicago's "Ten Year Plan to End Homelessness," emphasizes preventive measures, permanent housing rather than shelters, and long-term support services. Research shows that people respond better and are more successful in rebuilding their lives when their living situation is secure. That peace of mind is invaluable.

This is something Inspiration knew all along: Treating people with dignity and respect makes a difference. The other night I was eating dinner with Shiriony and another guest. The guest was immersed in his pain, telling us over and over about all that he'd lost. His job. His home. His belongings.

Shiriony listened attentively and then said, "You'll get more and it will be better. But it can't come to you until you let go of the other first. You have to let go of what you lost before the goodness will come."

The guest looked Shiriony straight in the eye and said, "Thank you."

That's the cafe. It's a place where people never thought they'd be, in situations they never dreamed of, and yet they come in, break bread with one another, and feel human.

Homelessness is a condition, not an identity.

• • •

During the two years I wrote these stories, I checked facts on occasion and researched details when needed. Mostly, I focused on the themes, the repeated messages, the moments when their voices changed, became deeper, passionate, more emotive. The moments I knew they were speaking their truth. The truth as they knew it. As they lived it.

What surprised me most is that in every interview, without fail, the wisdom or insights I most needed at that moment in my life came to me. At first it unnerved me, but as it continued, I began to think of it as grace. I'd simply smile and say,

"Thank you. I needed that reminder."

I needed to trust, even when I wasn't sure of the outcome. Or I needed to remember that I'm not alone. Or to think about how people are the most important resource we have. That experience has been a great gift in my life. It makes me realize how interconnected we all are, and how we need each other in ways we have yet to fully understand.

You can still find me on Friday mornings at Inspiration Cafe and either Wednesday evenings or Sunday mornings at The Living Room Cafe. Those who know me best know I'm not a particularly cheery or chipper person at 7:00 a.m. But mornings at the cafe are different. Even though I've usually only been awake for forty minutes, the cafe brings out something wonderful in me. I am transformed into "Ms. Mary Sunshine," as my mother used to tease me as a child.

The truth is I am simply living into hope.

• • •

My hour commute from work usually ends with me zooming through a freeway underpass about four blocks from my home. The radio's blaring and my thoughts are racing through my to-do list for the evening.

About three years ago, I happened to notice an amalgamation of blankets under that same freeway underpass, on the narrow ledge where the slanted concrete meets the freeway. And down below, I saw two or three grocery carts parked on the sidewalk.

It terrified me to think that every night I passed by such tremendous need and didn't know what to do about it. How could that be? I thought about leaving food. Everyone told me I'd be in danger. I did it anyway. But an hour later, I felt just as unsatisfied as I had before. Nothing had changed.

But then one morning, I was sitting with Michael Purnell in the cafe and I decided to ask him what I should do. He'd been homeless. He must know. So I launched into my dilemma. He listened closely, nodding occasionally. I told him I'd been taught to always acknowledge the person, to smile, to say "Good morning," to look the person in the eye.

"But what is that in the scheme of things?" I asked.

Michael smiled, took a sip of his coffee, and then with great tenderness said, "Never underestimate what a 'Good morning' will do. When I was out there, I was dead to myself. I didn't think I existed. But you say 'Good morning' to me, and then I think, 'Hey, I must still be here. I can't see me. But you see me. So I must still be human.'"

About Inspiration Corporation

As long as we as a society continue to put the acquisition of material wealth above human dignity, we will always have poverty and we will always have homelessness. We're really just putting our fingers in the dam.

– Christopher Persons
Executive Director, Inspiration Corporation

• • •

Inspiration Corporation serves more than 1,600 people annually. Its mission is "to help men and women who are affected by homelessness and poverty improve their lives and increase self-sufficiency through the provision of social services, housing and employment training in an atmosphere of dignity and respect." Their programs include:

Inspiration Cafe and The Living Room Cafe are two therapeutic communities where guests (participants) and alumni (graduates) enjoy meals that are prepared and served by volunteers in a restaurant style. Guests also receive individual case management and referrals to community services, housing, education and employment. Inspiration Cafe was founded by Lisa Nigro in 1989. The Living Room Cafe was founded by Jennifer Kihm in 1995 and merged with Inspiration Corporation in 2003.

The Healthy Living Program addresses wellness issues. Programs include, among others, men's and women's groups, health workshops, yoga classes and Alcoholics Anonymous meetings. Art for All involves group outings to cultural and recreational events, while Dream Big provides tutoring and after-school programs for children at The Living Room Cafe.

The Alumni Services offer ongoing support for graduates, including access to cafe programs, eight meals a month, access to a food pantry, and alumni newsletters and reunions.

The Housing Program provides subsidized housing for up to twenty-eight participants at one time. These studio and one-bedroom apartments are within walking distance of Inspiration Cafe and The Living Room Cafe. In addition, the Housing Locator Program identifies affordable private market housing opportunities for clients of Inspiration Corporation and several other social service agencies.

Employment Preparation Training is a four-week work preparation course offered at various shelters throughout Chicago. The training is a part of The Employment Project that merged with Inspiration Corporation in the summer of 2005. The Employment Project also offers case management, employer outreach, job placement and retention services.

Community Voicemail System provides individual phone numbers and twenty-four-hour free message retrieval for clients of Inspiration Corporation and social service agencies throughout Chicago. This service makes securing employment and housing opportunities much easier.

Cafe Too is a culinary job training program and a restaurant open to the public. The twelve-week program is open to guests, alumni and job seekers outside of Inspiration Corporation.

The Weekend Engagement Center is a daytime shelter offering a warm environment, group activities, laundry and shower facilities, bag lunches, and open case management. The Street-to-Home Initiative, in partnership with Heartland Health Outreach, provides services to unsheltered homeless men and women.

Over seven hundred volunteers support these programs. Inspiration Corporation also receives financial support from corporate, foundation and individual donors as well as the Chicago Department of Human Services, the Mayor's Office of Workforce Development, and the U.S. Department of Housing and Urban Development.

To become a guest, individuals must obtain a referral from another social service agency and complete an application process. Admission requirements include being drug and alcohol-free for at least thirty days, having no recent history of violence, and demonstrating a willingness to work toward obtaining housing and employment.

About the Front Cover

Photographer Steven Gross donates his work every year to Inspiration's Art Auction, an annual spring fundraiser. Known for event, portrait and editorial work, Steven has been featured on *Good Morning America* as well as in *Esquire* and the *Chicago Magazine.*

One morning, over ten years ago, Steven and a group of media photographers volunteered to cook breakfast at the cafe. He's been hooked ever since, donating more of his time as well as serving on the board of directors. When I ask him what keeps him coming back, he's quick to answer, "The people."

. . .

Quantreel Taylor prepared the meal featured on the front cover. A graduate of Cafe Too culinary arts training program, he enjoys working as a sous-chef for the restaurant. He was part of the inaugural staff.

Notes

Introduction

1. Statistics on the homeless population are from Chicago Coalition for the Homeless, "The Facts Behind the Faces," Winter 2004-2005. The count of homeless men and women on a given night in Chicago was conducted by the Chicago Continuum of Care in March 2004.

2. Inspiration Corporation is comprised of Inspiration Cafe, The Living Room Cafe, Cafe Too and the Weekend Engagement Center. The Weekend Engagement Center is located four blocks away from Inspiration Cafe and next door to Cafe Too. Open Saturdays and Sundays, the center offers group activities, bag lunches, clean showers and case management.

Chapter One: Fortitude

1. Cafe Too is an intensive culinary arts training program. In addition to learning cooking techniques, students hone their restaurant service and job-readiness skills. They prepare and serve dinner to guests and alumni at Inspiration Cafe, and meals to the public during their internship. Classes begin every eight weeks and are currently twelve weeks in duration.

2. In May 2004, severe weather and heavy rainfall caused widespread flooding over northern Illinois. The Village of Gurnee was declared a state disaster area.

Chapter Two: Generosity

1. The Single Room Occupancy (SRO) program was authorized by the McKinney-Vento Homeless Assistance Act. It offers rental assistance to homeless men and women in conjunction with the rehabilitation of the space. Tenants pay a portion of their income, typically thirty percent. The rental assistance payments from the Department of Housing and Urban Development make up the difference as well as compensate owners for some rehabilitation and maintenance costs.

2. Supplemental Security Income (SSI) is a federal income supplement program. Funded by tax revenue, it helps elderly, blind and disabled individuals who have little or no income. It also provides funds to meet basic needs for food, clothing and shelter.

3. The application process for Cafe Too includes a math and reading proficiency test. Applicants must be homeless, at risk of becoming homeless, or low-income.

4. Excerpt read by Jose Contreras is from *How to Turn Failure into Success*, written by Harold Sherman (Upper Saddle River, New Jersey: Prentice Hall, 1982).

Chapter Three: Forbearance

1. The minimum wage in Illinois is $6.50. As of August 2005, the federal minimum wage is $5.15.

2. "Reach Out and Touch (Somebody's Hand)" by Diana Ross. Written and produced by Nickolas Ashford and Valerie Simpson, Motown Records,1970.

Chapter Four: Humility

1. Inspiration Corporation provides subsidized housing for participants. The studio and one-bedroom apartments are within walking distance from Inspiration Cafe and The Living Room Cafe. Participants pay thirty percent of their rent and after two years, that money is returned to them for future housing needs.

2. Quotes from Samuel Smiles and Krishnanurti in Shiriony VanChilds' narrative are found in *A Guide for the Advanced Soul*, written by Susan Hayward (Australia: Hayward Books, 1984).

3. Grant sponsored by the Mayor's Office for Workforce Development.

4. Quotes from Winston Churchill and Leo Tolstoy in Shiriony VanChilds' narrative are from *World Tribune*, the weekly Buddhist newspaper published by Soka Gakkai International.

5. Volunteer In Service to America (Americorps*VISTA) is a full-time, year-long domestic volunteer service program created in 1964 as part of the "War on Poverty." Americorps*VISTA volunteers serve in a wide variety of nonprofit and public agencies in urban and rural communities. They receive educational vouchers in return for their year(s) of service.

6. The Chicago Continuum of Care is a consortium of over two hundred service providers, advocacy groups, foundations, faith-based organizations, government agencies, and homeless men and women, which implements Chicago's "Ten Year Plan to End Homelessness." The plan, "Getting Housed, Staying Housed," prioritizes prevention, permanent housing and wraparound services.

7. Chicago Alternative Policing Strategy (CAPS) is a community policing initiative that brings the police, community members and other public agencies together to help identify and solve neighborhood crime.

8. According to the Chicago Coalition for the Homeless, a minimum wage full-

time job is insufficient for a family to pay fair market rent for a two-bedroom apartment. This is true for every state in the U.S. They also report 166,000 people experience homelessness in Chicago annually.

9. Pacific Gardens Mission is the "oldest, continuously-operating rescue mission in the country." Located on South State Street in Chicago, Pacific Gardens Mission was founded in a small storefront in 1877.

10. Rest Shelter is an overnight shelter. Founded in 1971, Chicago Uptown Ministries continues to serve the neighborhood through a variety of means: a food pantry, counseling services, a learning center as well as summer camp, Sunday worship, and much more. And Heartland Alliance is a human rights organization dedicated to serving the needs of the most vulnerable in our society.

Chapter Five: Love

1. Inspiration Cafe was founded in 1989 by Lisa Nigro.

2. Charlie Frankel volunteers Friday mornings to cook breakfast. Seafood omelets with hollandaise sauce have been one of his many specialties for the past fourteen years.

3. Illinois Department of Children and Family Services.

Chapter Six: Responsibility

1. T cells are a subtype of white blood cells that have an important role in immune function. HIV attacks Cd4 cells and drops the count. Anything below 200 puts you at high risk for infections that do not affect people without HIV or other immune deficiencies. Bi-low is the viral load, the number of copies of the virus per milliliter of blood.

2. On March 11, 2005, a man was escorted into an Atlanta courtroom for his trial when he stole a deputy's gun and shot and killed the deputy, the judge, and the court reporter.

Chapter Seven: Compassion

1. Genesis House offers a long-term residential program, daily crisis center, court advocacy and outreach program for women trying to escape prostitution and homelessness.

2. Organization of the NorthEast [O.N.E.] is made up of eighty community organizations that are committed to building and sustaining a diverse, mixed-income community on Chicago's northeast side. O.N.E. initiatives include afford-

able housing, education, homelessness and immigrant rights. The organization celebrated its 30th anniversary in 2003.

3. Laura Singer was the previous executive director of The Living Room Cafe. When The Living Room Cafe merged with Inspiration Corporation, she became the director of housing.

Chapter Eight: Trust

1. Emmaus Ministries is an evangelical ministry of Catholic and Protestant Christians that reaches out to men living on the streets who are involved in sexual exploitation.

2. The Cuentos Foundation creates and facilitates cross-cultural art programs. "Art giving voice to the stories of our diverse communities" is their mission.

3. *Journal of Ordinary Thought* publishes personal reflections on everyday life. The *Journal* aims to be a "vehicle for reflection, communication and change."

4. Scrap Metal Soul's spring 2005 show was entitled, "The Heart of Our Souls: Stories of Urban Lives."

Afterword

1. Statistics on the housing crisis and working homeless are from the National Coalition for the Homeless, "Why are People Homeless?" and "Who is Homeless?" Fact Sheets, June 2005.

2. Causes and types of homelessness are found in *Beside the Golden Door: Policy, Politics, and the Homeless*, written by James D. Wright, Beth A. Rubin, and Joel A. Devine (New York: Aldine De Gruyer, 1998).

Acknowledgments

M y deepest gratitude goes to all the men and women of the cafes for welcoming me and graciously allowing me to be a part of something far greater than I ever anticipated or expected over the past three years.

Every week, with great warmth, you invite me to break bread—to listen to your stories as well as share my own. You have changed me for the better and blessed me with a far deeper appreciation for the abundance in my life, both tangible and intangible.

To those who have walked this journey with me, I cannot thank you enough. To the classroom teachers—Sandra Bridges, Susan Stanula, Rodney James, Debbie Caserio and Lori Cantor—for getting me to talk about writing, and to their beautiful and lively students whose writing brought back my own. To my mentors and colleagues in the field of education—Sara Spurlark, Janice Preston, Sarah Machamer, RaShone Franklin and John Rodgers—for encouraging me to listen and heed a new calling. And to my friend, fellow educator and recent author, Jordan Sonnenblick, thank you for carrying the torch and lighting my path when I most needed to see.

A special thank you to Christopher Persons for all his support. To Lee Nagan and Amy Davis, for giving the book a new home. To Rosalie Riegle, for being a trusted writing companion. And to all the writers who graced my life with encouraging words, guidance, and books that inspired me: Studs Terkel, Neenah Ellis, Julia Cameron, Jonathon Kozol and Elizabeth Ann Stewart.

To my fellow artists and dear friends, Emily Swindell and Delia Rico, thank you for being honest and insightful readers. To Pamela Bird, Michele Choe, Angela Neglia and Karin Norington, thank you for reading my heart and reminding me to stay the course. And to the men and women of my centering group, thank you for keeping me grounded and inspiring me by your example.

A special thank you to all the chefs for their delicious recipes. They are the perfect garnish for the stories. Thank you to the Inspiration staff for answering my endless questions, and to Steven Gross for capturing the essence of the cafe through his camera lens.

To the Friday morning cooks—Charlie Frankel, Jon Heuring and Penny Simmons—thanks for making me laugh so early in the morning and giving me the best breakfast I get all week. And to all those who offered a suggestion just when I needed it most, among others, Katie Brick, Cynthia Brown, Nic Dasovich, Mary Jo Huck, Hillary Krantz, Michael Kuhn, Rose Nash and Tamara Wood, thank you.

An ocean of gratitude to my mom, an artist herself and the best last-minute editor a daughter can have. We do make a good team, in more ways than one. And to my dad, who supports me in all that I do. To the rest of my family—my brothers and sister-in-laws, my nieces and nephews—thank you for never doubting.